What Does it Mean?
Selected Writings 2006-2013

Menachem Creditor

"Not everything we do is a fulfillment of the divine will, but everything must be measured by the divine will, and everything is either a response to or a retreat from it. ...I am worried about only one thing. Do we look as we believe we should look in terms of the most authentic interpretation of our heritage? You and I are rabbis, and [one] who fails to live up to [their] designated role is *Kovesh Rabbanuto* – [a suppressor of their own rabbinate]."

> Rabbi Gerson Cohen, *Proceedings of the Rabbinical Assembly (1980), quoted by* Rabbi Gordon Tucker, *in "Can a People of the Book also be a People of God?"*

in memory of Helen Dubin *z"l*

CONTENTS

Israel

Judaism

Introduction

It was early in my rabbinic career when this all began.

As the first assistant rabbi in a lovely and loving Jewish community in the suburban Boston enclave of Sharon, Massachusetts, my roles and responsibilities were a work-in-progress. Which meant that I was afforded something precious and rare for a pulpit rabbi: *the space and time to experiment.* That might not have resulted in my engagement, as a writer and activist beyond the Jewish community, were it not for a series of intersecting events.

This is what happened:

One day in late 2003, a colleague called to ask for my signature on an ad in the local Jewish newspaper in support of LGBT Marriage Equality for Massachusetts, already signed by 40 other rabbis. I agreed. This was something new for me, but I didn't give it a second thought: I believed in this cause. I was simply joining my name to those of other rabbis who did too.

But that's not how it felt to everyone in my synagogue community. It surprised them that their newly-minted rabbi would take this specific stance in the public sphere. (I hadn't thought to talk it over with my senior rabbi nor the lay leadership of the synagogue. *Newbie mistake.*)

When members of my synagogue community saw my name in the Jewish papers in support of Equal Marriage, responses were varied. Many didn't even bat an eye. Some were excited, even proud. Some were deeply offended.

The president of the synagogue came to share his concerns at not having been consulted, and said to me, "We didn't know we were hiring an activist."

My sincere response those many years ago still makes me smile. I asked, *"What's an activist?"*

I meant the question. The difference between Jewish values articulated in a sanctuary and Jewish values articulated beyond the synagogue building was, to my untested rabbinic mind, an illusion. After all, I had studied the *midrash*:

> *What do we learn from the Torah's instruction that the Ark of the Covenant be gilded with gold not only on the outside, but also on the inside? That a person's inside should match their outside. (TB Yoma 72b, adapted)*

I saw my signature in the paper no differently than the sermon I had given the Shabbat just before. The synagogue president disagreed. And he was far from alone. Heated debates, emotional outpourings, public debates, and further media attention forced me to reflect with some urgency upon the question I had naively asked the president: *What is an activist?*

I hadn't given thought to the politics within my shul, nor to the way my stance on a big question would impact others. That was short-sighted. The graciousness of my senior rabbi and the vibrant diversity of community members turned this political mistake into a moment of deep learning and reflection surrounding about methods of communication and rabbinic leadership. More than that, it enabled me to grow into the role of rabbi-activist, and to better understand the inevitable pushback from congregants who disagreed. (*A lesson every rabbi never stops learning.*)

Sometimes pushback was gently communicated. *Sometimes not.* And, many times, these heated exchanges left me with a need to let it out, to express my deepest feelings on whatever issue we had debated.

And so, in a loving and diverse supportive synagogue, I explored what it meant to be a rabbi beyond the synagogue by writing. *A lot.* I wrote about issues of social justice, Israel, Jewish Pluralism, parenting, life-moments, and culture. I wrote in Jewish papers, on my own blog, and then in others, including the Huffington Post and The Times of Israel.

Collecting these essays now is an act of hope that they might help others consider offering their own voices as builders of the world around us, a world in deep need of collaboration and inspiration.

Some pieces included in *What Does it Mean* are ones I'd write today. Some are not. I've preserved the original, raw essays, in order to demonstrate a discernable unfolding of one rabbinic voice.

(To be honest, sometimes I can't remember that I wrote what I'm reading. To bare a little more of my soul, sometimes I am truly shocked to hear my younger self say something I've only recently, painfully, learned. As Dr. Who might say of this, it feels somewhat *timey wimey.*)

I owe so much, and remain deeply grateful to the community and leadership of Temple Israel in Sharon, Massachusetts, for guiding me well, for empowering me as my voice emerged. And to the sacred community of Congregation Netivot Shalom in Berkeley, whom I've had the honor of serving for the last 10 years, my gratitude runs deep. *Thank you all.*

To the One who is beyond time and within every second, Lifeforce that flows in and between us all: *Thank you.*

> Menachem Creditor
> Berkeley, CA
> Sivan 5777 / May 2017

Reflections

Eternity Can Wait

Certain moments grab hold of you and demand attention. They are unpredictable, volatile, and magnetic. Once encountered, they are forever. But they are also ephemeral. They are not meant to be endured, nor are they, in a real sense, "real." These moments of "Eternal Return," of some yearned-for primal experience are inherently about alternative timelines. They are only alive in the past and in the future. There is no present for a mythic moment — it is too attached to Eternity to be limited to 'now.'

This is "Mythic Time."

Trying to live in Mythic Time is like trying to breathe in a Mikvah, a ritual pool for personal transformation. The sacred womb of water envelops, holds, caresses, transforms, invites, offering everything always. But it is not endurable. It is not a place of engaged living. It is a liminal space, a threshold. Immersion in Mikvah is a consuming, frightening, bare, illuminating encounter with Eternity. It is a disengagement from the world.

Mythic Moments, liminal encounters, are not meant to last. But they are tastes of Eternity, of boundarylessness. They are steps out of life into Heaven, but they are too charged to be helpful in an ongoing way.

Liminal space is 'not here nor there.' And attempting to live in the Mythic moment is the same as ignoring real moments in time, real opportunities and obligations and relationships - missing the person before you in the name of swimming in boundarylessness.

In the World to Come there are no distinctions, which is literally Divine. But, in this life, we are called to Live fully, to be present in every possible immediate moment.

Liminality is only for visiting. It is a hint of the World to Come.

Eternity can wait.

Today is real and right here.

What Does It Mean?

In Dara Horn's 2006 work of spiritual fiction *The World to Come*, she portrays Marc Chagall and the enigmatic Yiddish poet Der Nister (The Hidden One) as teachers at a Ukrainian school for Jewish orphans. Der Nister sees a blue painting Chagall has just completed and asks "What does it mean?" Chagall's response is mystifying: "*It means blue.*"

When texts, headlines, and faces are searched for deeper layers of significance; when disease and tragedy are "explained" by survivors and those who would be comforters; when we, in our helplessness as observers, try to fill up the void that inevitably follows loss — that is when we forget that sometimes meaning is exactly what we feel: *blue*.

There aren't always redemptive answers. How can we possibly explain the death of a young person? The death of any person? When we say *kaddish*, are we truly extolling God as "*magnified and sanctified*"? Are we instead standing with Allen Ginsberg who composed a radical and original *kaddish* for his mother, writing:

> "*Toward education marriage nervous breakdown, operation, teaching school, and learning to be mad, in a dream — what is this life?*"

Are we saying what we mean?

Stating the pain, accepting a comforting hug —
screaming "Oh God!" — they "mean" the
emotions behind them. Saying *"baruch dayan
emet"*, a ritual blessing, incomprehensible in its
literal translation "blessed is the Judge of truth",
when we hear of someone's death is not an
answer, not an explanation, not a justification.
These rituals — the hug, the crying, the blessing
— they are useful even while not expressible
meaning. They force us to hear our own voices,
to recognize that we have a body, to know that
we're not alone. But they mean *"blue."* They
mean *"happy."* They mean *"sad."*

I sat on a *beit din* (ritual tribunal) recently,
witnessing the spiritual rebirths of individuals,
young and old, as Jews. As soon as I emerged
from the *mikveh* (ritual bath), I heard news first of
an attack in Israel and then of the death of a
precious young person.

Mikveh/birth, life/death.

What does it mean?

As soon as we emerge from our own birth
waters, we experience the cold air, the unfamiliar
bright lights, heightened vulnerability. Life is not
soothing.

The world-controllers of Aldous Huxley's *Brave New World* pacified their inhabitants with a powerful drug called "soma," taken to escape pain and bad memories through fantasy. And there are moments where fantasy does sound a whole lot easier than the worries of our world. But life calls, bringing unsolicited rapture along with complicating pain. Being born is not easy. Horn writes:

> *"What does a child resemble while it waits in its mother's womb? As a boy, Der Nister had been taught the answer: a folded writing tablet. Its hands rest on its temples, its elbows rest on its legs, its heels rest on its backside, and a lit candle shines above its head. And from behind eyelids folded closed like blank paper, it can see from one end of the world to the other. There are no days in a person's life that are better or happier than those days in the womb. When those days must end, an angel approaches the child in the womb and says, the time has come. But the child refuses — wouldn't you? (Didn't you?) Please, the child begs, please don't make me go. And then the angel smacks it under the nose so that it falls from the womb and forgets — which is why babies are always born screaming. But before that they are happy, and they wait. (The World to Come, p. 81)"*

We are not handed happiness in this world. But we are not purposeful before we are born.

Each of us has that angelic impression under our nose. Each of us experiences moments of jolted memory, blinded again by the candle we saw through closed eyes, called back to consciousness by shocking events, both happy and sad. These moments mean just that: happy and sad.

Blue... Gold... Sunsets...

Life is too precious, too full of unfolding remembering to willingly miss.

As Horn writes, "The World to Come *will come.*"

Perhaps the goal to set is to not lose ourselves in a search for meaning beyond Life.

Perhaps God is most present when all we can mean is what we are.

Perhaps, in this way, we strive to feel less alone, day by day.

The Eyes Have It

Beyond the physical process of observation there is the experience of "seeing."

This thing called seeing includes, among many things, perceiving, knowing, understanding, and interpreting. Stephen Covey's teaching is therefore essential: .

> *"Two people can see the same thing, disagree, and yet both be right. It's not logical; it's psychological."*

One thing can be seen in as many ways as there are observers. Not only must we ask how can "the truth" of any experience be communicated to someone who wasn't there; we must pause to consider whether fellow observers can communicate even with each other, given their inherently different impressions of the shared happening?

And it is urgent that the world considers these questions, as politicians and political forces increasingly claim clarity, and castigate "others" who don't see the "obvious truth."

As Paul McCartney and John Lennon put it in 1968:

> *"Try to see it my way / Only time will tell if I am right or I am wrong. / While you see it your way, there's a chance that we might fall apart before too long."*

"Before too long" feels frighteningly soon. There is a difference between varying visions of the world and power-seeking human beings with competing absolute-truth-claims. The former is akin to the ancient rabbinic teaching that at Mount Sinai everyone heard a different voice of God, and the latter is a tragic misperception of the universe, one which easily gives way to physical violence.

We must try to imagine the world through someone else's eyes. But is that even a possibility?

The first step towards sharing varying experiences of the world is the acknowledgement that your eyes are different from everyone else's. The truth as you experience it is no less true that someone else's. Some label this approach relativism, typically used as a discrediting term. But even "relativism" means many things, including the helpful concept that truth is always relative to some frame of reference.

My very make-up, both physical (my eyes) and meta-physical (my heritage), determines what and how I see. But looking straight into someone's eyes transcends particular frames of reference. Eyes are beyond language, beyond culture.

As Emanuel Levinas wrote:

> "...those eyes, which are absolutely without protection, the most naked part of the human body, none the less offer an absolute resistance to possession..."

It is precisely the eye's nakedness that causes meeting another's gaze to be such an intense and inescapable moment of communication, beyond what even the best-chosen words can communicate.

As Norma Desmond, the silent-film star in Andrew Lloyd Webber's musical "Sunset Boulevard" pours out:

> "No words can tell the stories my eyes tell / Watch me when I frown, you can't write that down / You know I'm right, it's there in black and white / When I look your way, you'll hear what I say."

We glimpse, through the eyes of another human being, their soul. And we are forced to stop. For in catching a glimpse of another's soul one ultimately recognizes not their own soul, but rather an inherently kindred (yet, vitally, differentiated) reflection of the Divine Image. I see not myself in your eyes, not even you, but rather the possibility — *the reminder!* — that I and you are only two fragments of the Truth. When I am exposed to the Raw Source of It All, how can I but see that there is more to the universe than my sense of rightness?

I am so afraid when someone looks into my eyes. *They see me.* The only way to protect my vulnerable self is to hide from the world the Divine within me by closing my eyes.

But I'd rather take the chance of seeing and sharing with someone else something beautiful, something unpredictable and grander than what I can imagine with my eyes closed.

What is it About Bedtime?

What is it about bedtime? On the one hand it's an in-between moment: Daylight is fading, eyelids are drooping — a gentle goodnight seems natural. On the other hand, there is the "simple task" of getting a child to bed, tucking them in, and finally going to take care of "grown-up stuff." How difficult it is to preserve this escapable sacred experience.

And yet, if we rush we miss the very first "I love you too." We miss seeing in our child's eyes an emerging understanding of the world. We miss the blindingly holy uniqueness of this independent person if we look away too quickly. And it's so easy to be distracted.

What roots us in the moment? Ritual. A hug, the *Shema*, a shared story. The gift of saying Shema with a child is inestimable. No ringing cell-phone is worth answering when you and your child are truly present with each other. There is nothing to accomplish, no way to fail.

All there is is wonder.
Grandeur.
Love.

And why limit this practice to parenting? Imagine the power of looking into the eyes of a loving partner, a beloved friend and saying the Shema. So intimate, and such a relief from the tumult of the world. It's just easier to talk about seeing Infinity in a child's eyes, perhaps because they haven't come to feel limited by the burdens of adult life and a challenging world.

Every one of us, old or young, has the same eyes we did as children. They've just seen more. Internalized a world that is so much, too much, with us. We miss the sunset because it feels so far away. Not the child. Childhood is a time when we can draw an elephant being swallowed by a boa-constrictor, give the moon a hat for a gift, delight in an echo, and know for certain that wisdom lives inside ourselves.

In that moment when we say the Shema, we are children once more, effortlessly testifying to the infinite oneness as we bid each other goodnight.

A World Without Children's Voices

The very beginning of Exodus includes the following familiar narrative:

> "A certain man of the house of Levi went and married a Levite woman. The woman conceived and bore a son; and when she saw how beautiful he was, she hid him for three months. When she could hide him no longer, she got a wicker basket for him and caulked it with bitumen and pitch. She put the child into it and placed it among the reeds by the bank of the Nile. And his sister stationed herself at a distance, to learn what would befall him. (Ex. 2:1-4)"

The power of Moses' birth is largely lost when read in the context of his rescue by Pharaoh's daughter. Once we realize that his birth immediately follows Pharaoh's declaration that every male child born be thrown into the river (Exodus 1:22), the act of a certain man and woman of Levi gains in significance.

In fact, says the Midrash:

> "... when Moses' father Amram learned of Pharaoh's order, he immediately divorced his wife Yocheved (their names, as well as Miriam's, are absent from our text).

Miriam said to her father, "Father, your decree is worse than Pharaoh's! Pharaoh only issued a decree that the males should die, while your decree applies to both males and females. Pharaoh decreed that the children's lives be terminated only in this world, and you have decreed that they not live both in this world and the world to come. Pharaoh is wicked, and the likelihood is that his decrees will not be fulfilled. You are righteous, and your decree will certainly be fulfilled!" (Ginzberg, Legends of the Bible, p. 287)"

Miriam's prophetic chutzpah led to her parents' brave decision to bring a child into a threatened world.

During a recent Winter vacation week, I visited both a mall and the Boston Children's Museum and considered both their very different environments and the very similar people who frequent them. The noise of each was almost deafening, with voices ricocheting off walls and windows. Both places contained "hands-on" and protected areas. Both were protected from the elements beyond their defined boundaries. And found within both were omnipresent children and caregivers.

It occurred to me, as I watched young face after young face pass by, that every child's face was also the emerging face of a potential parent. The training provided to these future parents' in each space was vastly different. The mall teaches that acquiring things is exciting. The museum teaches that interacting with the world is fun. The variety of colors and flavors at the mall is actually a barely-hidden mask of material uniformity.

Every *thing* has a label. *And a price.*

The inability to avoid looking at someone else in the museum while experiencing newness is more deeply experienced as an explicit statement that learning alone is less than learning together.

Both the museum and the mall serve as gathering places. But the mall leads me to escape the noise. The museum encourages me to listen and learn from the sounds.

Having recently experienced Cormac McCarthy's novel *"The Road"* and Alfonso Cuarón's film version of P.D. James' novel *"Children of Men"*, I feel renewed urgency when I hear children. Almost desperation.

I am afraid of the observation one of the characters in the film shares:

> *"As the sound of the playgrounds faded, the despair set in. Very odd, what happens in a world without children's voices."*

It's not my spiritual perspective as a father that prompts these thoughts. Nor is it my fear that either McCarthy's devastated landscape or James' youthless world will actually come to be.

I am simply concerned that we adults all too often miss our obligation and opportunity to see our children as emerging parents. When we program for Shabbat morning, do we nurture the caregiver aspect of our children's development? When we pass by a homeless person, do we remember that they too were one of those noise-making children? Do we acknowledge the bravery of today's parents, who struggle so often with infertility, and who have chosen to bring children into an uncertain world, answering every dark headline with the birth of new soul?

Just imagine for a moment what our world would be without our Miriam's. We'd forget how to be parents. This is not the world for which we work.

Our world, our precious fragile world of dreams and laughter will only be realized when we remember to learn from children and publicly celebrate our parents. Childhood lasts such a short time today, with omnipresent media and commercialism. Let's not miss it by creating separate space for our children. Let's find ways of dancing together to the noise of their laughter.

Then Miriam's redemptive chutzpah will be fully present again.

Upon the Death of an Enemy

Immediately upon returning from our community's *Yom HaShoah* commemoration tonight, I was greeted by the news that Osama Bin Laden, *Yemach Shemo veZichro*/May His Name and Memory Be Erased, had been killed by U.S. forces in a mansion outside the Pakistani capital of Islamabad.

From the immobility of being a Jew confronting the Shoah, the worst disaster our People has ever endured, I was shocked into the confusion of once again being the New Yorker I was nearly ten years ago, in shock, afraid, and helpless to do anything in the face of the worst assault on the United States in its history.

Which emotion is the right one? Is there a "right" one? Can there be only one in a moment like this, when we remember as Jews our 6 million during the Holocaust and we remember as Americans the almost 3,000 people killed on September 11, 2001? How do we respond when the architect of enormous evil is brought to justice? What does it mean for us, as Jews, and as Americans, that Osama Bin Laden has been killed?

According to a Midrash, when the angels rejoiced at the victory of God and the deliverance of the Children of Israel at the Red Sea, they invited God to join their celebration. God declined, saying, "How can I rejoice when my children are drowning?" God's response, as intuited by our tradition, teaches us that the very people who enslaved and tortured us were still human beings when viewed through sacred eyes.

But a human being, an irrevocable Divine Image, is not immune from Justice. When the trial of Adolph Eichmann, which lasted off and on from April of 1961 to May of 1962, ended with Eichmann's execution, Rabbi Martin Cohen remembers being told by his father that *"the entire Jewish people was having a party that day."* Rabbi Cohen goes on to say, *"I'm not sure I knew what he meant. Maybe I did. Probably not."*

I'm not sure what I mean right now. I'm relieved that an evil has been eliminated from the world. I'm mourning our lost Six Million. I'm watching the crowds on Pennsylvania Ave and Ground Zero, weeping at all that happened and is forever changed, aching for some healing and some small amount of hope. I'm still hearing the testimony from a Shoah survivor shared less than three hours ago echoing in my heart, proud to have joined as a large Berkeley Jewish community to bear witness to our collective pain. I'm lost right now. That's all I think I can mean at the moment.

We do not rejoice at the death of our enemy. The implementation of justice is not a joyful celebration. As Rabbi Cohen writes of watching the recording of Eichmann's trial,

> *"In this man's eyes are reflected the ghosts of his uncountable victims...and also nothing at all."*

I am riveted by the face of Bin Laden. I do not want to look into his eyes. Those eyes witnessed the snuffing out of so much life; those eyes remained willfully blind to the pain and loss he caused. I believe justice has indeed been served today. Joylessly, as is appropriate.

May America know a measure of comfort after these almost 10 years, and may we redouble our efforts to rebuild our Nation in a more unified way, knowing that this incredible pain has been felt by members of every political persuasion.

May the Jewish People bear testimony to the attempted Destruction of our People by redoubling our commitment to building and supporting our Jewish communities, knowing that every moment of Jewish Living is the ultimate legacy of those who died *Al Kiddush haShem*, for the Sanctification of God's Name.

May our vulnerable world sleep a little easier tonight.

Amen.

Justice

Restoring the Arc (of A Love Affair)

The prophet Isaiah is on my mind and in my heart more and more. His voice rings in Yom Kippur's Haftarah reading with messages I fear we've forgotten. With messages I believe we must begin to remember, even if they hurt our hearts. Especially because they hurt our hearts so deeply.

Isaiah's words call out to us through the years:

> *"Thus says God: I dwell on high, in holiness, yet also with those with low in spirit, reviving their hearts. ... The House of Israel seeks Me, like a nation that does what is right, saying 'Why, when we've fasted did You, God, not see? Why, when we starved our bodies, did You pay no heed?'" [Isaiah 57:15, 58:1-3]*

God's answer through the prophet?

> *"Why?! ...Your fasting today is not enough to make your voices heard on high! Is this the kind of fast I wish for? A day of starving your bodies, bowing your heads, wearing sackcloth? Do you call that a fast?!*

This is the kind of fast I wish for: unlock the fetters of wickedness and untie the cords of the yoke. Let the oppressed go free and break every yoke. It is to share your bread with the hungry, and to take the wretched poor into your home. When you see the naked, clothe them! DO NOT IGNORE YOUR OWN FLESH!" [Isaiah 58:3-7]

Before we dare relegate Isaiah and his ancient words to the dustbin of history (though the inclination to forget what is right before us is understandable), let us say out loud what is true in our own community:

- 1 in 3 children in our county faces the threat of hunger.
- 22 assaults and domestic violence incidents and 2 shooting deaths occurred during the last few weeks here in Berkeley. To our great distress, this doesn't make us any different from any other place.
- Roughly 24,180 people have died from guns in the United States since the Newtown shootings.
- 1 in 5 children in the United States live in households that struggle to put food on the table.

And, of course, it's so much worse than that. These last weeks we've watched our country struggle not to ignore the flesh of our sisters and brothers in Syria. *Their very flesh.* Their flesh is our flesh, and we should be writhing in pain, not out of sympathy, *but because their flesh is our flesh.* The difference between us and them is a terrible misperception.

I know, I know. It's too much. Too heavy. Too much to bear.

But I'm begging you: *Please don't close your eyes.*

Yom Kippur demands your open eyes. Today is not the birthday of the world. Today's job is a lot harder. Today we look at our post-creation world, and it can be hard to keep our eyes open. Even harder to keep our hearts open. It's going to hurt. So that's how we'll start: by not pretending it doesn't hurt to actually see the world the way it is.

And looking won't be enough. You can cry your eyes out, and nothing will change. The way we'll stay strong long enough to do something about it is by remembering the words of the ancient sage Ben Hei Hei, who taught us "*Lefum Tzara Agra,* according to the pain is the reward."[Pirkei Avot 5:21]

If that is the case, then there is an immense reward waiting for the whole world somewhere in the future. *May it be so.*

You might think these problems push Isaiah's dreams of Justice into heaven, too distant to reach. But I say to us all tonight that they are not in the heavens. They are so very near to each of us. So very close. The solution is in our mouths, in our hearts,[8] if only we could remember it, restore it, so that Isaiah's vision wouldn't be so far away any more.

A story:

> *A few weeks ago, I drove into San Francisco for an AIPAC High Holiday Rabbinic sermon seminar. We spoke about our obligation to strengthen our homeland, Israel.*
>
> *We discussed the Jewish obligation to respond to threats both existential and physical to our People's welfare. We spoke with profound and painful urgency of ongoing Jewish vulnerability in today's complicated world.*
>
> *In between statements of very-real Jewish fear, we ate danish and drank Peet's coffee. We communicated with colleagues and friends around the country via satellite, beaming our meetings to and from Washington, D.C., where we have access to our country's political leadership. Some more than others, everyone around the table had enough money. And all of us were white.*

> *I had to leave the city early, as I was scheduled to work back in Berkeley with some board members of American Jewish World Service, another meeting shared by well-off white Jews. And while our conversation was going to be about Jews doing righteousness in the world, a theme I will return to in a moment, I want to share something that happened in the space between those scheduled encounters:*

> *I was driving toward the Bay Bridge, and looked to my left. I saw a man pushing a shopping cart full of pekelach, small bundles. He was wandering, wearing rags, clearly homeless. And I had to pull over because suddenly I was crying. I stared through my tears at this man, because I was suddenly shocked into the realization that, between me and him, he was "the Jew."*

And so tonight, my dear friends, tonight I am asking each of us individually and all of us as a community to begin to remember what it is to be a Jew in the world.

A story, this one told in the name of Rabbi Abraham Joshua Heschel *z"l*:

> *Once there was a schoolboy who like many of us, would wake up in the morning and forget where he put his things the night before. So, one night, before going to sleep, he devised a solution to his problem.*

Before he got into bed, he took a piece of paper and a pencil and he wrote himself a note: "My eyeglasses are on the table next to the bed. My pants are on the chair next to the table. My shirt is draped over my pants. My shoes are on the floor under the bed. My socks are in my shoes. And, I am in the bed." He placed the list on his bed-stand and he went to sleep.

The next morning when he awoke, he took his list from his bed-stand and to his astonishment he found everything on the list. But, when he came to the last item - "and, I am in the bed," he looked at the empty bed and asked himself, "So, if I am not in the bed, then where am I?"

My friends, we have lots of lists of where our things are, because many in this room are blessed to have lots of things.

We are like, as Paul Simon put it:

One and one-half wandering Jews / Free to wander wherever they choose / Are travelling together... / On the last leg of the journey / They started a long time ago / The arc of a love affair...

We are just so very blessed. Feel the concern pulsing in this room right now. Know that we live in extraordinary times. We are Jews, free to be Jews. We are citizens whose voices matter in a constitutional democracy. The chair of the Democratic National Committee is a Jewish woman and the United States House majority leader is a Jewish man. Our Jewish ancestors yearned to be a free people in their own land, and today we have one.

Our list of miracles and accomplishments could go on and on, and I know we do not take them for granted. *At least, not most of the time*. Perhaps we've had it too good for too long to remember how things were, WHO Jews have been within history. *We forget.* That's completely understandable. It's not intentional forgetting.

And that's why we list *chata'im shebishgaga*, unintentional sins, in our prayers for Yom Kippur. We've become, through the journey we started so long ago, wandering Jews, now free to wander wherever we choose. We did not intend to forget to be Jews in the world, but we have largely forgotten.

Danish, coffee, freedom, and a homeland can do that.

But it is time to do Teshuvah, to Return to who we really are.

We're not in bed. We're not dreaming. We're in the real world, and as our teacher Rabbi Alan Lew put it so perfectly: *yes, this is real, and we are completely unprepared.* But we stand a chance if we open our eyes and wonder where we are and where we might be. And if we succeed, we might even fulfill the prophecy at the end of Paul Simon's song:

> *One and one-half wandering Jews / Return to their natural coasts / To resume old acquaintances / Step out occasionally / And speculate who had been damaged the most / Easy time will determine if these consolations / Will be their reward / The arc of a love affair / Waiting to be restored*

The arc of our love affair, a love that calls us as Jews in the world, is waiting to be restored. Our Jewish communities value davening and learning and Jewish continuity, caring for each other when we are ill, when we die; we embody a beautiful radical welcome. We are queer, we are straight, we are old, young, and in between. We are Jewish and not. We have members who have survived abuse. We have members who have financially and physically lifted our communities from the depths of collective imagining into reality. That's a whole lot of love. *But it isn't enough.*

Until we stand our ground and see every human being as worthy of the miraculous beauty we celebrate in each other's eyes in our synagogues, it isn't enough.

It will never be enough until wickedness is gone, until all the oppressed go free and every yoke is broken. Just because the Messiah hasn't come yet doesn't mean she isn't in the room with you right now, and in every room in every home and on every street, just waiting for someone to recognize the humanity and the divine spark in her eyes.

And before you think that I'm speaking at you and not to myself, let me borrow from Yom Kippur's language and confess my own sins. My story might sound trivial, but it is in my eyes every second:

> *A few months ago, I was trying to finish my work and get home in time to prepare for Shabbat. The shul's copy machine was broken, and so I had to run across the street and make some copies. I was rushing, too fast probably, coffee spilling, copies to make, and the Prophet Elijah appeared in the guise of a homeless person I had met a few times before and he asked for my help. But other things were more important. The Messiah could have come that day, but it wasn't important enough to even slow me down.*

I wish that were a singular event in my life, but it isn't. And, for me, it stands for something quite urgent in the world. I valued the coffee in my hand and the copies I could make more than the human being before me. *Et Chata'ai ani mazkir hayom.* I acknowledge my sins right now.

I was wrong. I sinned when I didn't even look the person in the eye. I forgot God in his eyes and, through that lack of care, diminished God in my own.

We look at Syria and Gun Violence and human trafficking and hunger and poverty and we forget, because remembering hurts too much, the refracted images of God involved. *But the flesh we ignore is our own.*

Isaiah isn't done with us, and we've got work to do. I'm asking you to please do this work as a holy communities, as righteous communities. We don't agree about God, but we agree that doing right is a mitzvah, a command we dare not ignore. Because our liberation, as Lilah Watson famously said, is bound up in every other's.

Two questions that matter quite a lot:

The first is: *What keeps you up at night?*

Pour it out. we're in this together. Our shuls are groups of loving people. We care about the world in different ways, but we support each other unconditionally. We're family. The pain any of us feels is pain all of us feels, and the way we'll mobilize to answer larger wounds in the world is by naming our own.

The second question is: *What gifts can you bring to support your community's effort to engage and heal the world?*

You have the opportunity to organize, to market, to pray, to fundraise, write, sing, teach - and the most precious gift of all - to give of your time.

When we know what strengths we can marshal as a community, we will miss fewer opportunities to act righteously. When you have the power to do something that needs doing, it is your responsibility. We have it in our power to be righteous, and we therefore are obligated. Be a leader in your community and be righteous!

A week ago, I was privileged to collaborate with my dear friend and colleague Rabbi Jason Klein, in formulating a question asked of President Obama during a *Rosh haShannah* call from the White House to American Rabbis.

We asked:

> *American Jewish history has had waves of civic engagement, and in this moment of our nation's history, there is dire need for the repair of our social fabric, a "re-covenanting" of the American faith community to heal our urban communities. What is the role you, as convener-in-charge, hope we'll have in this urgent national task?*

The President's answer was to hand the responsibility back to us. What, he challenged us, would be the place of the American Jewish community in leading America to a better day?

Friends, our world is in need of our strength. And we have a lot of strength to offer. Thousands of people choose Judaism every year. Fair trade kosher items are emerging thanks to Jewish activism. *You might think that's not a big deal, but the slaves who make the other products don't think that way.* We convened Gun Violence rallies, staff food pantries, march with sisters and brothers for civil rights, and the list goes on and on, But these are gifts we've already begun to give.

But, deep in our hearts and our bones, we know it hasn't been enough yet.

Many Jews are reporting that davening these past holidays has been the deepest it's ever been. A friend explained it succinctly: *it just needed to be.*

Our communities are in and of the world, and we are hurting, and so our prayers have to be better than ever before. And they were. *Just look at the power at our disposal.*

I haven't been sleeping much these last weeks. And I have a feeling I'm not alone. This world of ours is not in great shape, and as soon as we think we're used to one crisis another rears its head. *So let's rear ours.* We are Jews in the world, and we've been slaves, and we've been exiled, and hurt. As Heschel taught us:

> *"In the realm of the spirit, only [one] who is a pioneer is able to be an heir."[Man is Not Alone, p. 164]*

So let's, together, demand an end to pain for all people. Heschel once again, pointed us in this direction when he said that "*the heart of human dignity is the ability to be responsible.*"

Dear God, we're going to try to remember not to be calm, not be silent, not to close our eyes.

Love us, Adonai, and help us restore the arc of our love affair, the very same moral arc of the universe your prophets Isaiah, Abraham Joshua Heschel, and Martin Luther King Jr, sang and shouted and cried over.

God, we're just groups of people. But we're also so much more. Look at the tears in our eyes and help us never miss the Messiahs on our streets.

And it's tiring to care so much, God, so we ask for the strength to love each other - and ourselves - as much as we're willing to love the world. Fill us with enough strength to make our commitments sustainable.

Adonai, we know we are required for the sake of the world to give what we can. Help us be strong enough to give what is necessary. We're here, and we're trying. Be with us please.

May this year be one in which our precious, fragile world - and every inhabitant - is judged for life, and for peace.

Amen.

Progress from Process

The keyboard I am typing on is not of my own making.

Processes beyond my sight (and ability) were involved in crafting this helpful thing. We all know, somewhere in the backs of our minds, that the food we eat, the clothing we wear, and the gadgets we use come from somewhere beyond our vision. It can be so easy to forget that they all, truly, come from one place: human labor. As a rabbi, I guide myself and others to offer gratitude to God and the Earth for every piece of abundance we are blessed to enjoy. But, regardless of one's theology, it is clear that the hands that bring things from the earth, assemble bigger things from smaller things, and that bring things from one place to another are human.

The awful truth is that, all too often, the human owners of these artful hands are treated like things by a faceless global economy, of which I and you and everyone else are part. Rabbi Abraham Joshua Heschel once wrote,

> *"A Process has no future. It becomes obsolete and is always replaced by its own effects. We do not ponder about last year's snow."*

Will we pause long enough to look at the objects we possess and see that what we think of as "process" is actually a chain of human beings? If not, then we participate in a criminal act of willful forgetting.

This is a lot to handle. *Heavy stuff.* And so I'll offer that I believe the question is not: "How can I be free of all this?" but rather, "What actions can I take today to help one person become one step closer to freedom from slavery?" Unseen people around the world will remain invisible until those with the luxury to worry about others become aware of the forced labor that pervades society — and do something about it.

Thanks to organizations like Fair Trade Judaica and T'ruah: The Rabbinic Call for Human Rights, these steps are closer to home than you might think. FTJ is building a fair trade movement in the Jewish community, and is partnering with T'ruah's 1,800 rabbis to promote Guilt-Free Chanukah Gelt, a (tasty, kosher) reminder of the freedom the Jewish people won many years ago.

Today, many young children are trafficked and forced into working on cocoa farms with no pay and in unsafe conditions in the Ivory Coast, where more than half of the world's cocoa is grown. Fair Trade Judaica's Guilt-free Gelt Campaign's goal is to draw attention to this issue and let people know that fair-trade standards prohibit the use of child labor. Thanks to FTJ's pioneering work in the Jewish community, and T'ruah's amplification of this prophetic call, we stand a chance at change.

This year, when we hold pieces of Guilt-Free Gelt in our fingers by the glow of the *chanukiah,* I pray one more person somewhere in the world, far beyond our vision, might similarly savor the sweet taste of freedom.

A Rabbinic Riff on Capitalism

Sparked By the Magnificent Philanthropy of J.K. Rowling

JK Rowling has given away about 160 million dollars.

That's a lot of good being done by one very good, talented and successful person. You might, then say that capitalism can be a redeeming force in the world. And while many do everything they can to change the world through the financial means they are blessed to achieve within a capitalist economy, this very meaningful good effort is inherently dependent upon the righteous conviction of the successful.

That means that capitalism must also be recognized as a "dependency system," in which the vulnerable need the powerful to give their wealth away. Yes, Capitalism can include powerful forces for good, but I remain unconvinced that it's an inherently good system. We should say about Capitalism what Winston Churchill once said about democracy: "It is the worst form of government, except all the others that have been tried."

A good system would eliminate vulnerability and destitution as a likely outcome, regardless of the goodwill of the few. Capitalism is not going away, and self-interest (the all-too-human basis for its global dominance, usually trumpeted as "individual rights") is here to stay.

I'm just saying that we shouldn't be so proud of free-will offerings.

A successful person of faith who lives in a capitalist society should use language like "obligation" and "responsibility" and "bearing the burden of the other" to describe their giving.

Heed the call
to end modern slavery
in our own backyard

On Sept. 22, 1862, President Abraham Lincoln issued the preliminary Emancipation Proclamation, setting the date for the liberation of more than 3 million black slaves in the United States. In it he wrote,

> *"And upon this act, sincerely believed to be an act of justice, warranted by the Constitution, upon military necessity, I invoke the considerate judgment of mankind, and the gracious favor of Almighty God."*

Looking back these 150 years later, we know that despite the considerate judgment of humankind and the gracious favor of the Almighty, the eradication of slavery is yet an unfulfilled mandate.

This past summer, I travelled with American Jewish World Service to Africa, where I was confronted by the brutal truth of slavery legacy in societies still infected with its presence. Embedded in communities and industries across the world, children are sold for as little as $50 into a life of forced labor, malnutrition and physical abuse. Young girls are trafficked into lives as sex slaves. My eyes have been changed by what I saw, the children I sang with, communities still touched by the enduring darkness of human oppression.

But I didn't need to travel across the world to see slavery. Here in the United States, T'ruah: The Rabbinic Call for Human Rights is mobilizing the Jewish community to fight slavery in our home communities and in the products we buy, including a ground-breaking partnership with the Coalition of Immokalee Workers to end forced labor in the Florida tomato industry.

I am guilty of knowing that slavery persists, all the while living a life of smartphones, food and clothing that are all touched or produced by slavery. And I am grateful to both organizations mentioned above, as well as others doing similar work, for their tireless commitment to continue raising awareness and leading the Jewish community to making the world a more just place for every person.

Let's do something about this. On Oct. 1, 2011, the Trafficking Victims Protection Act, the cornerstone of the U.S. effort to fight human trafficking, the largest piece of anti-trafficking legislation in U.S. history, expired as a result of congressional inaction and partisanship. Call your senators and ask them to support the Trafficking Victims Protection Act (S. 1301).

Benjamin Franklin's proposed great seal for the United States was a depiction of Moses leading the Israelites to freedom, a journey that commands the Jewish people to "treat the stranger who sojourns with you as the native among you, and you shall love him as yourself, for you were strangers in the land of Egypt." Every person, created in the image of the divine, is worthy of dignity.

Our story of slavery is older than the ones being written in our world this very day. And we can — we must — do something about it. As Americans, we are called. As Jews, we are called.

Jewish tradition teaches that *teshuvah*, repentance, is achieved only when we are confronted with the same wrong thing again and given the opportunity to act justly. I had to travel around the world to be reminded that slavery persists in my backyard. I intend to learn this lesson well and share its heavy obligation loudly.

The modern prophet Rabbi Abraham Joshua Heschel wrote:

> *"The image of the person is larger than the frame into which they have been compressed."*

Just imagine how high the heavens will have to expand to make room when every woman, man and child is free.

Righteousness, Justice, and Reuben Fulfilled

I've found the multiple roles of citizen and rabbi difficult to untangle, despite a deep personal commitment to the separation of Religion and State. It is inappropriate to use my status as a religious leader to push a particular agenda in a civic debate. But, as I've encountered social ideas being shouted in God's name, I feel compelled to step forward into the discourse, title and all, perhaps a necessary violation. As Ralph Waldo Emerson wrote in 1863,

> *"It is as impossible to extricate oneself from politics as it is to avoid the frost."*

Human Rights Shabbat, as sponsored by T'ruah: The Rabbinic Call for Human Rights and *K'vod HaBriyot*: A Jewish Human Rights Network, was designed to promote an authentic Jewish voice for Human Rights. For despite the extremely positive way Jewish communities speak of our dreams, our highest ideals, there is a serious gap between what we claim and what we do. One need only to look at our ancient Jewish narratives to see that historic Jewish aspiration doesn't always lead to action.

In Parashat VaYeshev (Genesis 37:1 - 40:23), what we would label "Joseph's Rights" are violated at least twice. He is sold as a slave (a condition which is all too alive today: 27 million people around the world are enslaved in forms of debt bondage, sex work, slave labor, and domestic servitude) and he is indefinitely imprisoned (which, despite the current US government's work to close Guantanamo Base, is the explicit policy of the current administration to continue holding prisoners without trial in Afghanistan).

These are rights, inalienable by any democratic government or king, which we, as a North American Jewish community, promote with our words. And we claim the Torah's and Jewish Tradition's moral authorities in our self-descriptions. But what do we actually do to addresses these violations of Human Rights?

A provocative *midrash* demonstrates this inconsistency with stark clarity. When Joseph's brothers plot to kill him (Gen 27:18-19), Reuben intercedes, saying

> *"Let us not take his life... Shed no blood! Cast him into that pit out in the wilderness, but do not touch him yourselves (v. 21-22)."*

But in the Torah's description of Reuben's actions, there is a clear inaccuracy: The Hebrew text says that Reuben "saved him" (v. 21).

We know this isn't the case. While his intention is explicit in the text ("to save Joseph from them and restore him to his father (v. 22)"), we see that Reuben leaves his brothers, returns, discovers saw that Joseph is not in the pit, tears his clothes, and says "The boy is gone! Now, what am I to do?" (v. 29-30).

He *didn't* save Joseph, despite the Torah's wording.

The Rabbis in *VaYikra Rabbah* suggest the following radical interpretation concerning the obviously false claim of Genesis 27:21:

> *"Reuben said [upon reading the Torah's account of his actions], 'If I had only known that the Torah would say that I saved Joseph, I would have done it.'"*

This is only too true in our communal and individual lives as Jewish, as Americans, and as Global Citizens. As President Obama stated in his Inaugural Address, there is a "price of citizenship." In using this approach, he actually stepped into a faith-based framework: There are no "rights" in religious tradition, there are "obligations." The Jewish concept of universal justice is Tzedek/Justice, wherein the individual in Jewish tradition is, has the right to expect, and is commanded to achieve Tzedek, as in:

> *"Tzedek Tzedek Tirdof / Justice, Justice, Shalt Thou Pursue! (Deut. 16:20)"*

The trickiest part of that approach is the notion of "commandedness." Not all of us believe in God. But then again, no one must. This is one of the supreme values of Judaism - ours is a non-dogmatic spiritual system for enhancing particularism in service of the universe. And the very language of our sacred text can meet us where we are, as a whole. God sits, according to Psalms, on *Tzedek* and *Mishpat*, on Righteousness and Justice (Ps. 97:2). Without human work to actualize Righteousness and Justice God is not present in our world.

It is up to us.

But there's just so much to do. Our world has so much need. Could we possibly eradicate slavery? Can we change the practice of indefinite imprisonment?

A famous Jewish legend involves the concept of the *Lamed Vavnikim*, the 36 righteous people without whom the world would cease to exist. When one of the 36 dies, another takes his place. But one of the definitions of a *Lamed Vavnik* is that they don't know that they are one of the 36. (Thinking you embody righteousness often gets in the way.)

The Jewish literary mind of Berkeley-based author Dan Schifrin recently presented an approach related to these figures that could change the very way many Jews (and others) see themselves. Schifrin weaves a parable of a young man who, upon learning the legends of the *Lamed Vavnikim*, decides to become one. He spends an entire day unceasingly helping people across the street, picking things up when people drop them, cleaning litter, until, by the end of the day, he just doesn't have any more capacity to care. His compassion is completely depleted. He just can't do it all.

Neither can we. But that's no excuse for not trying. We can find one area of advocacy, one of the things we've always claimed to believe in, and start the work. Today.

Reuben didn't fulfill his obligation, the one we know he believed in.

Will we?

Safe Jewish Homes

Years ago I spoke about Domestic Violence on Yom Kippur. Afterward, two very sweet members of my shul came up to me and said:

> *"Rabbi, you really shouldn't speak about such ugly things from the bimah. That kind of thing just doesn't happen here."*

To which I sadly responded:

> *"I'm so sorry to share with you that, two rows behind you and a little to the left, it does."*

Domestic Violence happens in Jewish homes. This is the reopening of a necessary conversation, because we need to talk about it. I wish we didn't have to. But it literally hits much closer to home than we'd like to admit.

The prophetic cycle is a theme within much of the Hebrew Bible. It goes as follows:

- God and the Jewish people are in harmo0ny,
- we stray,
- God gets angry and sends another nation to enslave us,
- we repent, calling out in our pain,
- God has mercy upon us and lets the Jews out from under the yoke of the other nation,

- and finally God and the Jewish people are in harmony.
- (Until the next time.)

Said differently, when the Jewish people cheat on God with another religion, God's jealousy leads to Jewish suffering, until the Jews submit again to a dependent relationship with God. Until the next time.

Much has been written about human relationship as metaphor for the relationship between God and Israel. And the implications of this metaphor are amplified a hundredfold in the words of this classic rabbinic interpretation, taken from *Midrash Rabbah* (commenting on Exodus 31:10):

> *When Israel was driven from Jerusalem, their enemies took them out in chains, and the nations of the world remarked: "The Holy One, blessed be He, has no desire for this people, for it says, They are called 'rejected silver.'" Just as silver is first refined from its defects and then converted into a utensil, again refined and turned into a utensil, so many times over, until it finally breaks in the hand and is no more fit for any purpose, so were Israel saying that there was no more hope of survival for them since God had rejected them, as it says, "They are called 'rejected silver."*

> *When Jeremiah heard this, he came to God, saying, "Lord of the Universe! Is it true that You have rejected Your children? As it says, 'Why have You smitten us so that there is no healing?' (Jer. 14:19)"*

It can be compared to a man who was beating his wife.

Her best friend asked him: "How long will you go on beating her? If your desire is to drive her out, then keep on beating her till she dies! But if you do not wish her to die, then why do you keep on beating her?" The man replied, "I will not divorce my wife even if my entire home becomes a ruin."

This is what Jeremiah said to God: "If Your desire be to drive us out of this world, then smite us until we die! But if this is not Your desire, then Why have You smitten us so that there is no healing?" God replied, "I will never kill Israel, even if I destroy My world!"

"...And it is not because," says God, "I am in debt to the other nations that I have handed over My sanctuary to them, but rather it is your iniquities that have caused Me to hand over to them My sanctuary. If this weren't the case, why would I have to do this?"

This cycle of theological abuse is difficult for many to accept, and rightly so. And linking God to jealousy and violent rage is not my goal. In fact, my goal is to demand the exact opposite stance - *that Judaism demands absolute rejection of all forms of abuse.*

We've suffered too much abuse in our people's history to cause it to anyone else.

The test of a community is the way it treats its most vulnerable. We, as a moral Jewish community, must reject any concept of God as a jealous and dominating partner, in part because it forces all of us to identify as victims. This is an unhealthy model of relationship, and a shameful, twisted image of a loving God.

But the abusive theological model and its language are found within Jewish tradition. We must take a next step together and acknowledge the fact that abuse has happened, and continues to happen, in traditional Jewish communities.

****

Abuse happens within Jewish families. Physical and verbal abuse happen in Jewish families.

We don't like to talk about what is ugly and painful. We feel shame in revealing our less than perfect family lives. We don't want the outside world to know. We don't want each other to know. We don't want to know it ourselves. So we remain silent. But we are hurting. Some of us are suffering, perhaps someone reading these words, in our midst. Others among us inflict deep pain upon those they claim to love.

Victims of abuse can be women or men, young or old, gay or straight. It has been suggested that, on average, Jewish women stay in abusive relationships for 5 to 7 years longer than non-Jewish women, primarily because they don't want to believe that Domestic Violence happens to Jewish women.

But: **Abuse does happen in Jewish families.** We've shared a text that portrays God as an abuser. We reject that depiction as evil and wrong.

But there are other aspects of traditional Judaism, present even in modern congregations, that maintain the weak position of the victim in the face of abuse. Here are two:

- *Some rabbis have invoked the Jewish ideal of "shalom bayit," of maintaining peace in the home, as justification for sending a woman back to her abuser. Some rabbis continue to counsel this way, and have only served to disempower suffering Jews. Perhaps worse.*
- *A get, or Jewish divorce decree, according to some streams of Judaism can only be issued by a man, who can torment his partner with the get's legal power and its control over the wife's future. This makes the vulnerable woman an "Agunah," a chained woman, trapped by Judaism's rules.*

These two aspects of traditional Jewish life are problems. They make victimization possible within Jewish families, they put families in danger, and they must be changed wherever they remain in practice.

We must take the deeply Jewish step forward and, together, condemn abuse of any kind in our community.

****

Abuse can be physical, sexual, verbal or emotional.

It can come in the form of the ongoing use of demeaning words like "you're stupid," or ugly, or crazy. It can be total access to and control over bank accounts and finances. It can be threats to injure children or pets. It can be monitoring and limiting friendships, going out, talking on the phone.

Domestic violence is not about having a bad temper or being out of control. It is about power and control - one person exerting power and control over another. Domestic violence impacts on the entire family, injuring also the children who witness abuse by hearing it or seeing it.

I offer two anonymous testimonies from Jewish victims of Abuse. One is physical, and might help those in verbally abusive relationships say, "Oh, that's not me." But the second is a case of verbal abuse, perhaps even harder to escape.

> *1) "The Jewish Community sees my husband as a respected professional who is educated, talented, outgoing, friendly, loving, caring, and compassionate. They were not witness to what took place in the privacy of our home. No one saw him hit, kick, and choke me. No one heard him tell our child, 'Mommy's dead.' No one was present when he threatened to commit suicide in the presence of our child, wipe me off the face of the earth, and promised that I would not survive the night."*

> *2) "I have a boyfriend who is charming to everyone, a real mentch, sharp thinker and everyone around looks up to him. So you can understand how I feel alone in how I am feeling - since everyone thinks so highly of him. It's difficult to talk to him about anything because everything I say is either "stupid" or "crazy". Sometimes I have to lie because I'm afraid of how he'll react to certain things. I don't mean to ramble - today was just a bad day. He says it's my fault that the relationship is going south. I know I have to distance myself from the relationship but, honestly, I don't think I can."*

We bear witness to these anonymous testimonies, wondering whether or not people near to us are in similar situations. We wonder, perhaps, what to do with the inescapable knowledge that there is, most likely, someone reading these words who is hurting.

To anyone suffering reading these words, I promise you that God loves you, God wants to comfort you, and God expects your community to help you. There are safe people to speak with all around the world. *You will be safe. You are not alone.*

So how do fulfill these promises? Jewish tradition offers clear guidance. The following is a brief summary of a lengthy teshuva, a Jewish ruling, by Rabbi Elliot Dorff, entitled "Family Violence"[1]:

> 1) Beating and other forms of physical abuse, such as sexual abuse, are absolutely forbidden by Jewish law.
>
> 2) Verbal abuse is absolutely forbidden by Jewish law.
>
> 3) An abuser has the responsibility to acknowledge his behavior and do *teshuvah*, repentence, by getting help.

---

[1] CJLS, HM 424.1995

4) Parents may never cause a bruise to their children, no matter what decisions they make regarding corrective parenting.

5) Children may not beat their parents, even when parents were formerly abusive themselves.

6) The requirement that one preserve not only one's own life (*pikuach nefesh*) but others as well, demanded by the laws of the pursuer (*rodef*) and of not standing idly by when another is in danger (*lo ta'amod al dam rayecha*), not only permit, but require others who discover spousal or parental abuse to help the victim report the abuse and take steps to prevent repetition of it. Jews who suspect that children are being abused must report such abuse to the civil authorities, no matter what the consequences. **Saving a life takes precedence over the presumption that parental custody is best for the child.**

These policies are binding. They are not optional. We are commanded by tradition to protect ourselves and to intervene when necessary for others. There are times when it is necessary to act to protect the vulnerable.

Now and always are those times.

****

Opening up darkened spaces is a scary, saddening task, but it is a sacred one as well. We've been taught by our tradition that

> *"anyone who saves one soul, it is said about her that she has saved a whole world."* [2]

There is nothing less at stake than the entire world of at least one person. And one person's safety is reason enough for us all to spend the energy talking about abuse.

Perpetrating violence on an intimate partner is an affliction with a spiritual dimension that threatens the welfare of the entire community. We act with commitment to the health of our community when we hold abusers accountable. We act in accordance with Jewish tradition's call to pursue justice when we declare that abusers cannot remain in our midst and must dwell outside the camp.

The fabric of a Jewish home is based upon the fulfillment of Jewish tradition's instruction to create spaces of safety. The fabric of our homes is our Jewish ethics, which demand that we pursue justice. The fabric of our homes is our prayer and ritual life, which call upon us to heal and create wholeness in our world.

---

[2] (TB Sanhedrin 37a)

For the welfare of both the individual homes we are blessed have, as well as the collective ones we create together, may we commit ourselves to doing so.

May God be with us, holding our hands, as we take these steps.

May our homes be safe - and healthy.

Marriage Ruling is about Universal Human Dignity

Massachusetts, 2002 — it was the first time I stood on the steps of a state capitol making good use of my right to free speech in support of equal marriage.

I was there as a civilian. I didn't feel it was appropriate to use my status as a rabbi to influence civic debate. But as I encountered hateful ideas being shouted in God's name, the example of Rabbi Abraham Joshua Heschel marching arm in arm with Martin Luther King Jr. pushed me forward.

I learned in Massachusetts that religious communities must be involved in civil debate.

California, May, 2008 — here we are again. With the decision of the state Supreme Court affirming that same-sex couples have a constitutional right to marry, we have taken a momentous step forward for civil rights.

I am proud to have served as part of this moment, addressing the San Francisco LGBT Center press conference on that historic day as a Californian, a rabbi, a Jew, as a human being.

I stood in front of the couples who were plaintiffs in this case, who put their lives on trial, and I wept. The joy shared by the thousands who attended that press conference and the countless others who labored for equal marriage in California was simply overwhelming.

But, as always, joy is fragile. The court's ruling has been dimmed somewhat by a campaign that threatens the decision with a hateful November ballot initiative that our Jewish community must denounce. The initiative is named the California Marriage Protection Act. Of course, all it protects is prejudice.

The initiative is an attempt to write discrimination into our state constitution. And without the involvement of the Jewish community, it stands a chance at passing.

We must see this issue for what it is: *a question of civil rights.* No matter how an individual Jew or a particular Jewish community interprets Jewish law with regard to homosexuality, the Supreme Court did not rule on Jewish law. It ruled on universal human dignity and equal rights among American citizens, regardless of belief.

But it is also important to acknowledge the arguments against equal marriage, and to be able to refute them. So here are some of the classic arguments found on sites such as Focusonthefamily.com and Protectmarriage.com. They are followed by responses.

• *Claim: The California Marriage Protection Act will protect the historic, natural definition of marriage.*

> **Response:** Rabbi Steve Greenberg, senior teaching fellow at the National Jewish Center for Learning and Leadership, has written, "Marriage is not a natural institution. Marriage is an institution structured by societies. All marriages are according to the laws of some communal body that honors them. They are a feature of civilization, not nature. Marking homosexual marriage as contrary to some natural laws is reminiscent of the justifications put forward in the U.S. for laws prohibiting interracial marriage."

> The very concept of marriage has, in Jewish history alone, included multiple wives and concubines.

• *Claim: A same-sex family is a vast, untested social experiment with children.*

> When opposing marriage equality in 2004, Boston Archbishop O'Malley wrote, "The citizens [of Massachusetts] know that such a law ... would inevitably lead to far-reaching changes in the institutions of our society, more importantly those which educate our children and grandchildren."

> Response: I pray that he is right. The real social experiment is how well we treat each other.

• *Claim: Equal marriage is a step down a slippery slope of relativism and moral weakness.*

> **Response:** Equal marriage is not capitulation — it is the embodiment of conviction and moral outrage.

> As the Progressive Jewish Alliance [now a part of Bend the Arc] wrote in its Marriage Equality Packet, "Jewish tradition is grounded in the principle that the law should be applied equally to all, citizen and stranger alike. We recognize and grieve the injustice perpetrated against gay men and lesbians — our members, family and friends among them — who are relegated to second-class citizenship when denied access to marriage, a fundamental institution of our society."

• *Claim: Marriage is for the purpose of procreation.*

> **Response:** We would never claim that couples who face infertility or who choose to not have children should not be married. While it is true that procreation is one of the traditional intents of marriage, same-sex marriages would not prevent such endeavors any more than heterosexual marriages require them.

As a rabbi who favors the extension of full rights to gay and lesbian and bisexual and transgender citizens in both civil and religious realms, I affirm the holiness of a shared union and believe in a God infinite enough to include the marriage of man to man, and of woman to woman, each the union of two divine images. The Torah, understood as sacred text, reminds us:

> *"not to oppress the stranger, for we were strangers in the Land of Egypt and you therefore know the heart of the stranger."*

The Torah, understood as the ongoing narrative of the Jewish people, challenges us in Leviticus with the overarching imperative to *"treat your neighbors as yourselves."*

This is a call to action. May we find the strength to respond with a deep Jewish passion for justice.

Culture

Dark Wisdom:
A Jewish Comment
on the Conclusion
of Breaking Bad

[*Spoiler alert.*]

Truth and beauty accompanied every devastating turn in the journey that was *Breaking Bad*. Perhaps even wisdom. As a religious devotee of Vince Gilligan's masterful narrative, I will be processing its conclusion this past week for some time.

What follows is one rabbi's commentary on a television show that was at once artful expression and transformative experience, pop culture and philosophy. Yes, it was dark. And yes, it was deep. We could do much worse than learn lessons of intention, truth and power by treading lightly through the complicated wisdom of *Breaking Bad*.

Breaking Bad was an excruciating show to watch. It was, at moments, hard to breathe through each passing scene. The pain of having its narrative flow interrupted by commercials would have been even worse. Thanks to Netflix and iTunes, I binge-watched my way through the entire series one summer, and watched only the finale "live." An attuned-ness to the characters' emotions, to the rich cinematography, to the terrible ripples of every action and word, undisrupted by distraction, was revelatory.

The Talmud instructs that *"one who connects liberation to prayer brings redemption,"*[3] a rhetorical way of making sure certain things are experienced in sequence and without interruption, so that engaged participants see that one intense moment needs and feeds off another, that distractedness gets in the way of flow. In this light, the very way in which we experience culture is a fascinating indicator of our ability to pay attention, to feel connected with just one thing. Jewish tradition calls this flow "kavannah," or intention. It's hard to achieve, but once you have experienced it, anything less feels like... well, *less.*

---

[3] Talmud Bavli, Berachot 4b, 9b

Walter White, the un-hero of the *Breaking Bad* saga, is a rationalist so skilled that, until the very last moments of the six-year journey, he even convinces himself that his evil actions are morally justifiable as each terrible one is taken, painstakingly mythologized as necessary for his family's welfare. White is compelled over and over to lie, cheat, murder, and hurt. But, as Rabbi Abraham Joshua Heschel wrote,

> *"an act is not good because we feel obligated to do it; it is rather that we feel obliged to do it because it is good."*

Only at the very end does White acknowledge was painfully true to every other character (and every viewer), which the writers had him say so simply:

> *"I did it for me. I liked it. I was good at it. And I was really — I was alive."*

This acknowledgement, and White's traumatized wife's (and our own) silent shock at its sudden blinding honesty, is one of the few lingering hints of redemption in a narrative arc that crossed countless moral lines. It is only through verbally naming our sins in the presence those we have wronged, Jewish tradition teaches, that we might reach forgiveness.

In Joan Didion's shocking *The Year of Magical Thinking* she explains her need to be alone after the sudden death of her husband:

> "I myself was in no way prepared to accept this news as final: there was a level on which I believed that what had happened remained reversible. That is why I needed to be alone."

This magical thinking leads to what playwright Henrik Ibsen called "*vital lies,*" defined by Daniel Goleman as "*soothing mistruths people let themselves believe rather than face the more disturbing realities beneath.*"

In this light, perhaps the most devastating moment of *Breaking Bad* occurs when White, exiled, dying from his cancer, reaches out in desperation to his son, grasping at one last chance to fulfill his delusional intention to support his family with ill-gotten financial gain.

White's son, finally exposed to the brutal consequences of his father's choices, just as brutally removes the illusion of righteousness from his father's eyes, breaking a myth of goodness masterfully woven and endured for far too long.

The blood on White's money is born from sin, a contamination irreversible even by the most skillfully woven lies. If only White had remained alone in exile, he could have gone on believing the lies. But we aren't made for such aloneness.

White never wanted to be alone, and so he is forced to reconcile his internal illusory self with the Walter White others know. It's a terrible confrontation, but it's also not good, we are told by the Torah, for a person to be alone.[4]

Power has been defined by historian Jon Meacham as *"the ability to bend the world to one's will, the remaking of reality in one's own image."* This is true goal of Walter White's work. He isn't in the money business, or the drug business, but in "the empire business." A Jewish legend of another empire-builder comes to mind:

> *After Hadrian, emperor of Rome, conquered the world, he desired to be declared God. Troubled after failing to become God, his wife told him, 'You can become God, for you are a great and mighty king, and everything is in your power. I suggest one thing: return God's deposit and you will become God.' Hadrian asked, 'What deposit?' His wife answered, 'Your soul.' When Hadrian replied that he was unable, his wife quoted the verse 'no person has authority over the day of death (Ecc. 8:8)' and told him 'in truth, you are a man, not God.'*

[4] Gen. 2:18

In an early episode of *Breaking Bad*, Walter White chooses the street name 'Heisenberg,' adopting his adopted namesake's principle of uncertainty. Is he good or bad, teacher or a criminal, avenging savior or angel of death? From the very beginning of the story, White has been dying and living, lying and, in his own way, tender and loving.

Whereas White isn't certain his dark choices will have been for nothing, we viewers are quite sure: his brilliant creators have given us much to ponder.

Found: A Jewish Reflection on 'Lost'

The French novelist Marcel Proust suggested that "the voyage of discovery is not in seeking new landscapes but in having new eyes." Nothing could better describe the television series *Lost* created by Damon Lindelof, J. J. Abrams and Jeffrey Lieber.

Through six years of creation and encounter, revolution and revelation, the characters of Lost discover not only the secrets of a mysterious island, but an unfolding of life before their eyes. With every disclosure of a previous encounter between characters whose only apparent connection was a doomed flight from Sydney, what became obvious was the truth of Rabbi Lawrence Kushner's notion of the "interconnectedness of all being," that swims in "an Ocean of God."

The difference between counting the waves and entering the glorious, glowing, unified whole is a matter of perception, of choosing to open (*or close*) your eyes.

Central, recurring experiences in Lost were expressions of central Jewish teaching: The facial expressions of the central characters of Lost at moments of awakening, of sudden awareness, were reminiscent of Emanuel Levinas' teaching that "Expression, or the face, overflows images."

The final season was the embodiment of the deep Jewish convictions that death is not forever and that every day should be lived as if it is your last.

And the question of a purposeful life couldn't have been more alive throughout the series. As Dr. Michael Berger has eloquently written,

> *Implicit in the notion of an intentional religious life is the assertion that religion makes claims upon us to which we must respond, that ... Judaism is able to teach us, challenge us, inspire us and elevate us — not just to affirm us. Admittedly, this may be at odds with our contemporary therapeutic American culture, where relevance to one's own needs and aspirations is often the basis for significance. But ... an intentional community is defined by some notion of ... disciplined performance with the promise of a higher, richer, more meaningful life.*

In other words, the pursuit of meaning begins with the prioritization of higher meaning over personal need, with the embrace of the notion of a calling, of *dharma*, of duty.

Most of all, it was by entering the eyes of the characters that the viewer experienced hints of redemption. As Levinas taught,

> "*the face the Other expresses his eminence, the dimension of height and divinity from which he descends.*"

The wonder of the universe experienced by each of the show's characters through the unfolding liminality of a mysterious island was, and remains, an opportunity for us to explore our own universes, wondering what it is that our eyes actually see.

Legacy and Family:
A Hadran for Harry Potter

[This piece was deeply inspired by J.K. Rowling's final installment of the Harry Potter series. There will be no spoilers here, but the emotionality of completing the book just now compels its own Hadran, its own traditional commitment to return and relearn its lessons.]

When my children's mother and I chose the names of our three precious babies, we were committed to naming them after family members we had loved and lost. It struck me immediately, when our youngest daughter was named, that the pantheon of my ancestral family was whole again. My Grandma *z"l*, my Sabbah *z"l* and my great-uncle *z"l* were alive again. There are simply no words for the burn in my heart birthed by their names. Naomi Shemer wrote in "Jerusalem of Gold" that saying Jerusalem's name is like experiencing *"the kiss of a Seraph."* A Seraph is a fiery angel. Shemer was so right.

I'm not sure what method for writing works here, and perhaps sharing this emotion so publicly is too much. But my family is alive. My family surrounds me. It's not just my eldest daughter's laugh, which reminds me so much of my grandmother. Or my son's eyes, which bring me right back to my Sabbah. Or the juxtaposition of my daughter's intense glances that make me stare again at her namesake's art proudly displayed in my home and office.

It is the deep knowledge — *even deeper than faith* — that their spirits are present, alive, learning and growing within my family again.

I am blessed. So incredibly blessed. Life is so full, so worth living, so worth sharing.

The traditional phrase "*HaMeivin Yaveen/One Who Understands Understands*" has always struck me as condescending. So let's *transfigure* it: May we all come to understand the power of knowing that those we've loved and lost are never truly gone. May we speak their names with smiles, with hearts overbrimming with gratitude.

Dynamic Connections: The Theology of 'The Runaway Bunny'

The children's classic "The Runaway Bunny," written by Margaret Wise Brown and illustrated by Clement Hurd, might seem an odd place to begin a theological reflection.

The Runaway Bunny begins with a young bunny who decides to run away: "'If you run away,' said his mother, 'I will run after you. For you are my little bunny.'" And so begins an imaginary game of chase. No matter how many forms the little bunny takes — a fish in a stream, a crocus in a hidden garden, a rock on a mountain — his steadfast and protective mother finds a way of retrieving him.

For a child who has ever tested the strength of a parent's love, this story offers both reassurance and challenge.

Brown's book asks its readers: How can the love of a parent for a child be explained, defined, demonstrated? The mother bunny responds to the many incarnations her child adopts, following him as he changes, not restraining his imagination while simultaneously (and doggedly) refusing to let him slip away. She changes along with him.

What do we believe?

Did the ancient Israelites who authored our holy
Torah, believe that God was describable, or
locate-able? Perhaps an answer may be found in
the dramatic and tragic moments when the
Jerusalem Temples were destroyed in 586 B.C.E.
and 70 C.E. For when we were exiled from our
land, carrying with us both the sights and smells
of a burnt Jerusalem and the dream of one day
finding home again, the rabbis created a new
midrash, a new vision of God's "location." They
taught that when the Jews were exiled, God's
holy Presence, the *Shechinah*, went with them.
"God adapted, morphed, changed along with
us," taught the rabbis.

Deep in the soul of the Jewish people is the
conviction that our *"Avinu Malkeinu"*, our own
"Mother Bunny," won't let us go. But the deepest
part of this is that we've never run away.

Even when we've rejected one image of God,
chosen one notion of the Sacred over another,
our relationship with God has remained strong.

For the Torah, God is an intervening character in
history.

For Rabbi Mordechai Kaplan, founder of
Reconstructionist Judaism, God is "the Power
that makes for salvation."

Definitions only accomplish so much, given their rootedness in limits of language. Words like Source, *Elohim*, Adonai, Spirit — all sublime pointers — affirm the infinite potentiality of the universe to be purposeful, to respond to the particulars of today.

I pray that we never run away from our Divine potential, that the challenge of belief is a compelling conversation we remain determined to share.

May our precious communities always feel the Presence of God.

And may the way we treat each other and the world around us always demonstrate the most sacred of ideals.

Wholeness and Sacrifice: Circumcision, Mutuality, Trees and Quilts

Shel Silverstein's classic *The Giving Tree* has, for generations, engaged children and adults while promoting a questionable message of sacrifice. A boy and a personified tree develop a relationship in which, as the boy grows, the tree provides for the boy's needs. Apples, leaves, branches — even tree-trunk — are given up by the tree to fill the boy's needs, until, when the boy is quite old, the Tree (who is really only a stump at this point) is only able to provide a seat for the boy, who accepts this final gift.

A more recent addition to the world of children's literature, *The Quiltmaker's Gift* by Jeff Brumbeau, tells a different story of sacrifice.

A king, who loves presents so much that he decrees himself two birthdays a year, desires a quilt made by a magical quiltmaker who only gives her stunning quilts to the poor. She informs him that with every gift he makes to someone else, she will sew one more patch of his quilt together.

His initial reluctance to part with any of his possessions gives way to increasing joy with every new opportunity to give, until the quiltmaker finds the king shoeless and happy, laughing on the forest floor with a poor child who is now wearing the king's former crown. When the quiltmaker presents him with his completed quilt, the king gives her his one last possession — *his former throne* — for her to sit on as she sews her quilts.

The striking similarity between the endings of the two books — the final gift of a seat — might help us reflect upon the stark contrast between the different journeys of sacrifice depicted in each book.

The Giving Tree contains a story of one-sided sacrifice to the point of injurious self-denial, perhaps not the message we would choose for our children — *nor for ourselves*.

The Quiltmaker's Gift tells of a different way of giving, one which leads to wholeness through potentially healing acts of mutual self-sacrifice.

A third story might beautify the tapestry.

In the Torah, we encounter the birth of God's relationship with Abram. God's first words to Abram are a command to:

> *"Go forth from your native land and from your father's house to the land that I will show you (Gen. 12:1)."*

We know nothing of Abram's life previous to this command from God to go to an unspecified place. Abram's willingness to set off on a journey with an unknown endpoint is perhaps testimony to the faith necessary for creating healthy relationship. This commitment is repeatedly tested through such moments as the banishment of Hagar and Ishmael[5], the binding and sacrifice of Isaac[6], and the command of circumcision.[7]

And it is this covenant (in Hebrew, *'brit'*; in Yiddish, *'bris'*) of circumcision that might most embody the Jewish journey toward healthy relationship of mutual sacrifice.

The biblical pre-amble is crucial:

> *"When Abram was ninety-nine years old, the Lord appeared to Abram and said to him, "I am El Shaddai. Walk in My ways and be 'blameless.' I will establish My covenant between Me and you, and I will make you exceedingly numerous...*

---

[5] Gen. 21:9-13
[6] Gen. 22:1-19
[7] Gen. 17:1-14

As for Me, this is My covenant with you: You shall be the father of a multitude of nations. And you shall no longer be called Abram, but your name shall be Abraham, for I make you the father of a multitude of nations.

I will make you exceedingly fertile, and make nations of you; and kings shall come forth from you. I will maintain My covenant between Me and you, and your offspring to come, as an everlasting covenant throughout the ages, to be God to you and to your offspring to come. I assign the land you sojourn in to you and your offspring to come, all the land of Canaan, as an everlasting holding. I will be their God."[8]

Two observations:

1. The word 'blameless' in English is an attempted translation of the Hebrew *'Tamim,'* a biblical word with many possible readings. One of the most commonly suggested meanings is its root, *'Tam,'* sometimes translated as 'simple,' as can be found in the four children section of the Passover Seder. Another connotation is found in the Hebrew phrase *'Tam VeNishlam,'* or 'whole and complete.' The command to be 'Tamim' might be most deeply understood as a command to become 'whole.' *How strange that the command to be whole is actualized through removing a part of Abram's body!*

---

[8] Gen. 17:1-8

2. It is certainly possible to read the above text quickly, knowing what follows. But when God says 'As for Me,' precious pathways to the sacred open. Jews are obligated to act in certain ways in order to fulfill our part in the covenant — *and so is God!* God might want to give us children, a land, majesty, and even God's Self ("*I will be their God*"), but God commits to a mutual relationship in which even God is vulnerable to the consequences of human action before being "allowed" to act in these ways.

In other words, people give up parts of themselves in order to become whole, and God must give up infinite freedom in order to enter into relationship with people. The lesson to be learned from the covenant between God and us is that true partnership requires each partner to sacrifice a part of self in order to make room for another.

The extremes of sacrifice are hazardous to the health of participant and partnership.

On the one hand is selfishness (no room-making for another), the other the loss of self (too much room-making for another) — both destructive to the relationship and to each of the independent selfs involved. As we learn from God's blessing to the very first human partnership, each partner must serve as an "*Ezer KeNegdo*," a helper ("*ezer*") and a challenger ("*neged*").[9] Both roles are necessary ingredients for healthy relationship.

Circumcision is not easy.

It requires faith that the future holds promise despite pain and belief that God is vulnerable to human action. And whereas we are viscerally aware of that which we give up for our side of the bargain, the Truth of God's sacrifice is not demonstrable. *It is a matter of faith.*

There are moments, such as circumcision, when it is hard to feel secure about God's commitment to humanity. But such is true about every relationship — there are moments in which we doubt an equal return on our emotional investment.

There are also moments when we are overwhelmed by the loving response of our partner. How *whole* we feel in those moments.

---

[9] Gen. 2:18

The only way to experience love is to make myself vulnerable to my partner. And so the challenge is to find a partner I can trust.

I believe God invites us to be holy partners, to learn to relate, to make space for each other and for the world.

I believe God is waiting for our response, waiting to be invited back into the world.

Israel

Reclaiming Zionism

This piece has been brewing for years. It is not a reaction to the well-organized Boycott, Divestment and Sanctions effort that in 2010, 2011, 2012, and 2013 (and many times since) struck the Bay Area, my hometown of Berkeley in particular. It is a processing of my experiences over the last five years as a Rabbi, a Jew, and a Zionist in the Bay Area.

The Zionism I embrace is Theodor Herzl's two-fold vision:

1) securing international legitimacy for the right of the Jewish people to a state of our own; and
2) actually building our national home.

This mission remains incomplete, and it is both everyone's and no one's fault. "Hawks" delegitimize internal critics. "Lefties" denounce rightist campaigns. Both distract the Jewish people from the greatest project in our collective history: *The State of Israel.*

How can a Jew today feel that they would not view the destruction of Israel as a personal tragedy?

Has half of our Jewish family forgotten the necessity of a home? Do we believe that "the wandering Jew" is a story of the past? I wish from my heart of hearts that this were true. It's simply not true yet.

And though the day might come, please God, when we can turn our Nuclear Submarines into underwater ploughshares, for now we need those shields. And while we are called to try not to use them, we are also called to have them at the ready.

Just 16 months ago, the Fogel family was massacred in their own home. Udi (36) Ruth (35) Fogel and their children Yoav (11) Elad (4), and three-month-old Hadas, may their memories be a blessing, were murdered by a terrorist. They lived in a settlement called Itamar in the West Bank.

There are Jews who compare their Israeli activist commitments with the motivation of the terrorist. It is an absurd comparison which comes along comments like "we have to question whether we should be mourning the death of the crazy uncle who is making things worse."

The Fogels were people I would have argued with until I was red in the face (and then some). But emphatic, fundamental disagreement is different from murder, and I weep and mourn for my lost sisters and brothers, no matter the deep differences with which we would have struggled together in life.

I am a liberal Zionist. That means I support the work of the New Israel Fund ("Say Yes to a Better Israel") and AIPAC ("Ensuring Israel's Security"). It means that, when I do criticize Israeli policies, I do so with a cautious and conflicted heart because I am talking about my home and about my family. It means that I sing the Hatikvah with tears in my eyes as I pray that "we have not yet lost hope, a hope of 2,000 years, to be a free People in our land."

There are those who suggest that our traumatic family history has rendered us unable to make ethical decisions. I disagree with this interpretation, but do hear it as a challenge to every side of the Jewish Israel conversation.

Can we embrace the numerous challenges Israel faces on behalf of the Global Jewish People, knowing that our disagreements are part of Zionism in-progress?

Said simply, is it possible for Jews who disagree to see each other as partners in building our people's home? This must be, I believe, based on "hawks" allowing for the dissent upon which democracy is built, and it must be based upon "critics" recognizing that their credibility must be based on explicit support for the State of Israel.

I am reminded of the teaching of Reb Nachman of Breslov, perhaps itself the ancestor of Herzl's vision:

> *"If you believe you can harm, then believe you can heal."*

Zionism also needs to come from the left — *right?*

One vignette demonstrates the lessons I learned at the AIPAC National Summit in Hollywood, Florida, some years ago.

Marc Ginsberg, a former U.S. ambassador to Morocco, presented a session titled "U.S. Outreach to the Muslim World." I had signed up for this talk, skeptical about the possible bias an American Zionist lobby might bring to this particular conversation.

Ginsberg began,

> *"There are 54 Muslim countries in the world. Twenty-two of them are Arab. Those two words do not mean the same thing, and we need to understand the incredible diversity in the Muslim world, country to country, and within each country, before we use words like 'Muslim' or 'Arab' to describe a situation. They simply aren't the same thing."*

This careful framing of the discussion surprised me. When I had informed colleagues and friends that I was to attend the AIPAC conference, they were surprised, given my typically liberal politics and the perceived hawkish tenor of AIPAC.

The myth that AIPAC has more in common with the tea party than my shul was shattered at the conference — as professionals, politicians and scholars, one after another, presented mostly balanced conversations about Israel, the U.S. and the world. I did disagree with many points, but I also learned that the stereotype I had accepted regarding AIPAC was wrong.

And then something else happened. As Ginsberg continued, he suggested that a healthy understanding of the Muslim world could begin with an analysis of Pakistan and Indonesia. No sooner had he said "Indonesia" than a participant in the front stood up, faced the room, and said, "*Obama lived there, you know.*"

That's when I got it. The problem isn't AIPAC. The problem is the American Jewish community.

AIPAC's mission is "to help make Israel more secure by ensuring that American support remains strong." But whose mission is it to educate the American Jewish community about its own proclivity to a worldview founded upon understandable fear?

It occurred to me that this question must considered side by side with the lessons learned during our local battles over Israel — on the U.C. Berkeley campus, at Berkeley's Peace and Justice Commission, at Richmond City Hall and at San

Francisco City Hall in recent years, over and over.

Those who attacked Israel through a well-coordinated divestment campaign said Israel disregards the plight of the Palestinian people. Israel's defenders largely focused on Israel's right to defend itself. The battles became a clash of "you're hurting them" versus "they're hurting us" — and the heated political climate ruined any chance of asking more important questions, such as: *"Whom do each of us dream to be?"*

Zionists (like me) who are prepared to publicly criticize specific Israeli policies are the ones with the problem. Whereas AIPAC publicly champions an unconditional Zionism as a strategic priority of the United States (which I support), many Israel-focused groups who lead campaigns critical of Israel's current realities abandon the word "Zionism."

That is the lesson, and these are the challenges.

This is a call to the New Israel Fund and to J Street, two organizations that resonate in my heart but are missing a crucial word in their public vocabulary: *"Zionist."*

When will the political left reclaim Zionism as an incomplete aspiration, acknowledging that its worthy work is part of the Zionist dream?

The New Israel Fund is "the leading organization committed to equality and democracy for all Israelis." That is the Zionism I believe in, the Zionism Theodor Herzl created with two goals:

1. securing international legitimacy for the right of the Jewish people to a state of our own; and
2. actually building the national home. Both goals have yet to be met.

Herzl's quote, *"If you will it, it is not a dream,"* demands the will to actualize such a reality — one that faces many challenges from without, as well as many from within. Israel's threats are not only outside its borders.

The increasing threat of Jewish fundamentalism in the Israeli government threatens Israel's soul, just as the threat of a nuclear Iran threatens Israel's body. But these are not "Israeli" concerns. They are Jewish problems, there and here.

When the only prominent organization using the word "Zionist" is not designed to further the internal Israeli enterprise, to foster the ongoing maturing of a Jewish democracy, there is something wrong.

Zionism is a Jewish dream, not the dirty word it seems to be recently.

Zionism isn't monolithic and it isn't easy.

Jewish dreams rarely are.

The Narrowing of the Israeli Mindset

I asked the following question of Michael Oren, Israel's ambassador to the United States, during his whirlwind trip through the Bay Area two weeks ago: Given the mandate for Israel, from both a geopolitical and traditional Jewish framework, to ensure the physical survival (*pikuach nefesh*) of its people, when is the right time to fight for Israeli religious pluralism for Jews?

Oren respectfully suggested that the American Jewish community should tone down its rhetoric when criticizing Israel's Jewish policies — in part because such criticism undermines Israel's claim to be the sole country that can be trusted with protecting religious pluralism in the Middle East.

His suggestion affirms, however, the need to keep the conversation going. After all, if the Israeli ambassador to the United States knows about the conversation and has to respond to it, it clearly is beginning to make a difference.

In Israel, where different sects of Muslims, Christians, Druze and Baha'i receive funds from the government, only one form of Judaism gets government funding. And Modern Orthodox (Tzohar) rabbis who are part of an effort to increase flexibility within Jewish tradition are typically criticized for sharing their opinions publicly.

There is a Conservative (Masorti) movement in Israel, but its 56 communities receive no funding from the government, and its ideals no doubt would be better served by a diverse group of Jewish leaders.

Israel's Jewish persona in the minds of many of North Americans is that it's a land solely for the ultra-Orthodox, which in turn has distanced us (*and our homeland!*) from our richly-textured heritage.

This point of view is even more prominent among young American Jews. According to a study released in January by two American professors, less than half of non-Orthodox Jews in the United States under the age of 35 believe that Israel's destruction would be a personal tragedy (compared to 78 percent of those over 65).

Worse than that, then-Kadima Party leader Tzipi Livni pointed to the measurable erosion of many young Israelis' Jewish identity. During a meeting with the Masorti Foundation Leadership mission to Israel, in which I participated years ago, Livni warned that if nothing changes, more and more Israelis will begin to think of themselves as Israeli and not Jewish.

David Ben-Gurion, the first prime minister of Israel, once quipped:

> *"We will know we have become a normal country when Jewish thieves and Jewish prostitutes conduct their business in Hebrew."*

Is this cynical vision of normalcy still our goal? Or has Israel — and we who love her — become "normal enough" to respond to a faltering national identity increasingly unaware of its own empty language?

The arrests and ongoing harassment of Women of the Wall and those on the ground in Israel fighting for religious pluralism demonstrate something worse than narrow governmental policy. Those actions represent the narrowing of the Israeli mindset.

Whereas once there were IDF induction ceremonies and coed school choirs at the Wall, today the enormously expanded *Kotel* plaza — and the small women's section — is part of what has evolved from a national site into a *haredi* (ultra-Orthodox) synagogue.

So much has the Jewish awareness of most Israelis shifted that when a participant with Women of the Wall was arrested a few years ago, Jerusalem police forcefully pushed her toward a nearby police station as she was holding a Torah. And when I met that person the following month, she said the police not only shoved her but also mocked her for wearing a tallit and holding a Torah.

We've been mocked before while holding the Torah. How can we be doing the mocking ourselves? Something has to change.

I recently met a winery owner in the Galilee who, in order to receive Israeli rabbinic kosher certification, is forbidden from touching his own grapes, machinery and casks since he is not Shabbat observant in a traditional way.

He is a deeply spiritual Israeli Jewish man who, despite his established commitment not to work on Shabbat, is subject to excessive requirements born from politics and designed to employ untold numbers of *haredi* ritual certifiers.

These requirements come at the expense of both Jewish and human dignity for many, and result in alienation from Jewish tradition.

If a Jewish woman were arrested in some other country as she tried to carry out a Jewish tradition, we would all — all over the United States — protest outside of the embassy. We would not give their diplomats a moment's rest.

We should do no less for and within our homeland.

Rabbi Shmuel Rabinovitch, the rabbi in charge of the Western Wall Heritage Foundation, criticized the Women of the Wall, who recently came to demonstrate at the Kotel after the arrests. He was quoted as saying, "The Kotel is a place of Jewish unity and should not be used to divide people."

Amen. Indeed, the Kotel is not a place for dividing people.

Judaism is more complicated than one form. May the place we all face become a welcoming meeting point for all forms of Judaism.

May the distinction of holding Torah be a point of dignity and pride for Jewish women and men, at the Kotel and everywhere else.

Judaism

In Defense of Jingle Bells

I awoke with a start that past Friday morning as I heard my then-5-year-old daughter sweetly entertaining her little brother with an almost perfect rendition of "Jingle Bells." It shocked me, and for reasons that might surprise both Jews and others.

When my daughter's teachers and I spoke about the musical selections within the public school afternoon program she attends, I learned that the list included songs painstakingly chosen for their "non-religious" content. Therefore "Jingle Bells" and "Frosty the Snowman" were in, while "Silent Night" and "Rudolph the Red-Nosed Reindeer" were out. On the one hand, I appreciated the sensitivity the larger Boston educational system employed when making this decision. But, on the other hand, I wondered if perhaps it isn't the best choice within reach.

When, also that year, a Seattle rabbi requested the inclusion of a Menorah in the holiday display of the Seattle-Tacoma International Airport, officials instead decided to remove the already-placed Christmas trees, choosing to respond with aggravated absence instead of reflective inclusion. That policy isn't where we should be headed. It would be a tragedy to prohibit any religious tradition from being shared. To paraphrase the classic ADL anti-hate campaign, "A Grinch against one is a Grinch against all." *No one wins on the day the music dies.*

Our goal should be a brilliant concert, with an orchestra as mixed as its audience.

Greetings like "Merry Christmas" and "Eid Mubarak" and "Happy Channukah" can, and should, be present - *and celebrated* - in the public sphere. Spiritual connectedness need not be based on one set of beliefs or practices, and the increasingly diverse ethnic identity of so many American towns makes each public sharing of a particular faith all the more important. (*Stores that recognize their diverse consumer base might present a healthy model worth studying.*)

How should we respond to the inclusion of an unaccompanied expression of a particular religion? Two options present themselves: the removal of music with specific holiday references (which includes Jingle Bells by association, I believe) and the introduction of various faith-related music and art. In other words, send it all away or bring it all in. How impoverished we would be to choose the first option. And how rich our society would be if we chose the second!

Consider how informed our children would be if they learned "*Takbir*" (with which the Fast of Ramadan ends) alongside "*Hark! The Herald Angels Sing*" alongside "*Rock of Ages.*" Envision the classroom, the colors decorating the walls. Just imagine the eyes with which our future leaders would see their communities, the dignity every one of us would enjoy. Our differences would help each person and sub-community see beyond itself. What a collaborative dream we could create, and what music we would sing!

Channukah celebrates the triumph of a small faith community over an imposing governing power. It is, in so many ways, the story of "us vs. them" which pervades ritual moments spanning the religious divide. When we recount to our children and ourselves the story of miracles, is the Festival of Lights one that only shines outward to the world? Do we implicitly judge the world as a place of darkness, where foreign tenets are stony and inert compared to our illuminated faith? There are important lessons of distinctness to be celebrated, but at what cost? Is it truly our dream to one day stand alone?

We must be brave. We must rethink our larger cultural narrative, so that every acknowledgment of particularity reflects an affirmation of the whole.

Chanukah and Thanksgiving (2013): It's Complicated

Much has been made of the overlap of Chanukah and Thanksgiving this year, a convergence that will not occur again for over 79,000 years. On the one hand, the meanings of the days are similar:

- Chanukah is a story of Jewish rededication, the Maccabees reclaiming contaminated sacred space, marking God's miraculous intervention in the military and ritual lives of our ancestors.
- Thanksgiving is an American story of bounty, gratitude expressed by formerly persecuted minorities, blessed to find home again through miraculous arrival.

But both these also narratives require of us, as American Jews, deeper and clearer thinking. Both holy days contain more within their stories than meets the eye, more than their ritualized re-tellings readily offer. The commonalities of these hidden, darker strata are also striking, perhaps even shocking:

- Chanukah is a serious challenge to the modern Jew, as comfortable (if not more) living as a global citizen than being seen as a Jew. Chanukah's notion of the "contamination of Jewish sacred space" is a code-phrase for Jewish assimilation, the natural dynamic of a Jew engaged in society, where the politics of identity easily make particularism uncomfortable. Only through the fanatic zealotry of the Maccabees, including the murder of fellow Jews who identified strongly with Greek custom, did the Chanukah story occur.

- Thanksgiving marks the Pilgrims taking of a land from its native inhabitants, one formerly marginalized group marginalizing another. Thanksgiving's celebration of "bounty and gratitude" forgets the Puritan's zealotry and their slaughter of those who already inhabited the "new" world. Only through the Pilgrim's fundamentalist world-view did the original Thanksgiving story take place.

The Maccabbees and the Puritans were zealots. Their violent thoughts and actions left a muddied legacy for Jews and for Americans. And, *gevalt*, my friends. We're both. How befuddling our sacred narratives can be!

What, then, are we to make of these days, these cold, dark days with contested, twisted narratives? How are we, as complicated modern Jews, to light our lights? What illumination pours through our windows into the world?

A popular Chanukah song goes as follows:

> "We have come to banish the darkness. / In our hands is light and fire. / Every one is a small light. / But together we are a mighty fire. / Out, darkness! / Run away before the power of light!"

Are we called, in the name of our cherished heritages, to shine brightly? *Without a doubt.*

Being a Jew is a beautiful gift in the world. Being an American is a blessing. Both come with weighty obligations, which are their very best parts.

Must we learn from our troubled pasts to never again deny others the brightest light of all: their dignity? *Without a doubt.*

Being a modern Jew requires the ethical use of necessary and hard-earned power, constant vigilance to stand in solidarity with the world's most vulnerable, remembering the oppressed stranger we've frequently been in history. Being a modern American means bearing responsibility — doing *Teshuvah* — for enduring American social policies and processes that have much in common with Puritans. An American wields the most noble of our nation's sacred ideals at no one's expense.

Can we be Jews in the world, proud and particular, and at the same time Global Citizens, pluralist and present?

Let's see if we can.

I think we've got that kind of Jewish power just waiting to be harnessed for the common good.

May this Chanukah and Thanksgiving truly banish darkness, bring bounty, cultivate gratitude, and challenge us to see the light in others' eyes.

Shabbat, a Cellphone, and Jewish Concern

I had a sermon fully prepared for Shabbat services. It was going to focus on the Exodus narrative and the Jewish implications of the biblical Passover sacrifice. *Then a cellphone went off during services.*

The cellphone rang during a particularly quiet moment of services, and the owner fumbled for a moment, so startled they forgot, momentarily, how to silence the sound. I counted to 10, and then walked over to the person, who was still holding their phone — a violation of traditional Shabbat norms in my community.

There was obviously nothing malicious about the phone going off, nor in the temporary difficulty its owner had in turning it off. And yet its sound tore at something primally important in our sanctuary: the essential "energy" of Shabbat, an antidote to the constant alarms of our hyper-connected technological age. Shabbat is a breath of uncluttered air in an infinitely distracting world, what the great Rabbi Abraham Joshua Heschel termed an "armistice with technology."

So that phone wasn't just a phone. It was an *"anti-Shabbat siren,"* brutally tearing Shabbat out of the very air. It was, therefore, truly difficult to contain my own disappointment at its invasion of our sanctuary, to temper my own fiery response to this weekday-contamination of Shabbat.

My carefully expressed words *"I'm sorry. You'll need to keep your phone off during Shabbat"* couldn't have masked the fire I felt in my own eyes. I saw this reflected in the phone-owner's eyes, and became instantly concerned I had violated one Jewish principle (human dignity) for the sake of another (Shabbat observance).

The *drasha* (sermon) I then delivered addressed a related idea: the dire need for more attention to be paid to particularly Jewish behaviors in the context of my shul community's deep and profound commitment to universal justice. The morning's Torah reading included the original Passover offering, the ritual of circumcision, the blood placed on the Israelites' doors just before the final of the ten plagues, and the command to teach every next generation that the liberation from Egypt is not to be understood as "freedom from bondage" but rather as, "freedom from slavery to now serve a holy purpose."

In other words, the role of these (and other) rituals is to affirm the particularly Jewish identity that today compels a Jew to act in solidarity with others.

We know what it is to be oppressed, and are therefore called to channel that experience into the commitment to being liberated with all people. As Heschel put it:

> *"The child becomes human, not by discovering the environment which includes things and other selves, but by becoming sensitive to the interests of other selves."*[10]

My message was a cautionary one, reminding a Jewish community of passionate activists that Jewish universal concern is rooted in Jewish self-awareness, in the embodied knowledge of our own story (including such rites as circumcision). In short, it is good to be good. But being good is not the same as being a good person who is a passionate Jew, manifesting our People's textured story, being fluent in, as my teacher Rabbi Jay Michaelson puts it, *"the vocabulary of our own souls."* [11]

Translated into deeply personal terms: *I am a human rights activist because I am a Jew. I am a human being because I am a Jew.*

---

[10] Man is Not Alone, 137-8
[11] Michaelson, Everything is God

Back to the unfortunate owner of that loud cellphone.

When services ended, there he was, waiting to speak to me. To be honest, I wanted to apologize for making him uncomfortable. The last thing I mean is to judge someone for a different pattern of observance, or for not knowing, or for a simple mistake. *Shul is meant to be a sanctuary from judgment as much as it is meant to be a shield from the incessant buzzing of the world.*

But when we found a moment to connect, and I offered my apology, he looked into my eyes and said,

> *"Not at all, Rabbi. I haven't ever really thought before about preparing myself for Shabbat, never taken the step of turning anything off so that I could be part of the Shabbat spirit. I'm grateful that this community takes Shabbat seriously enough to cultivate it. It was probably harder for you to find a way to communicate this with me than it was for me to hear it."*

Besides my deep relief at not having offended another person, I also felt an incredible affirming from his reflecting back the precious value of Shabbat.

It is said in Jewish tradition that Shabbat is meant to be *"a taste of the world to come."* This morning's experiences further convinced me that if we, as Jews, are going to help transform this world into the next one, then becoming fluent in the vocabularies of our own Jewish souls is a mandate worth strengthening.

I was reminded, thanks to our beautiful Shabbat this morning, that when self-awareness is intertwined with mutual concern, the world to come can feel just a bit closer.

A Rabbi's Christmas Thought (for Jewish Parents and Others)

As a *Yeshivah* high school student, I was told to not enjoy Christmas lights, "tainted" as they were by non-Jewish cooties. And, since I lived in a particularly lawn-happy neighborhood on Long Island, that meant ducking for cover every third house. The houses abutting my childhood shul were particularly hard to miss, with people driving from far away to witness a million-bulb spectacle, the carbon-footprint of which has yet to be determined.

When I got to college, though, something changed. First of all, the white lights adorning Columbia University's college walk didn't in the least resemble the garish ones I remembered. Secondly, I was done heeding the Jewish-insularists of my *Yeshivah* days. Most of all, I was a college student whose heart swelled with romance in the college air - what could be more romantic than the mystic lights on a cold winter night?

Which leads me to this thought.

We, American Jewish parents, guardians of the faith, have a choice. Do we try to diminish the magic of the lights our children see? We don't stand a chance. And, furthermore, *do we really not see the magic ourselves?* Are we afraid of Christmas voodoo? Or, are we secretly, deep down, happy to see the lights on these dark nights?

So, if we are not going to pretend to not enjoy Christmas lights, let's really talk about what's going on. *It's beautiful.* Human beings ache for a magic that illuminates the darkness, that shines goodness into a sometimes cruel world. We don't need, as Jews, to be afraid of beauty. In fact, the more we try to look away, the stronger the magnetic pull of Christmas becomes. In America, it's everywhere. Sometimes garish, sometimes classy, sometimes commercial, sometimes spiritual. It's just there. *Everywhere.* We live in it. And it can be very, very hard.

So here's the thought: It was a blessing this year (2013) that Thanksgiving and Channukah coincided, as reminder to not confuse Channukah's modest lights with Christmas' spectacle of the trees. If you are concerned that you and your children are become seduced by the lights, consider this: *magic is desperately needed in this world.*

Every Friday night and Saturday night Jews are called to banish the darkness with fire, bringing primal creative force into the world. Have you ever looked at someone else's eyes looking into the Shabbat candles' flames?

Shabbat is magic. Its cheer is waiting to pervade your home and your heart every week. The world needs more light, more spirit, more goodness.

So love it when you see it, and let your precious light shine.

Essays by Menachem Creditor
through May 2017

Driving to Shul on Shabbat & Holiness
The Times of Israel (May 11, 2017)

Why is Moses Kept Out of the Tabernacle?
myjewishlearning.com (March 9, 2017)

Joyfully Answering the Call
The Times of Israel (March 1, 2017)

Honor Our Dead. Build on Love.
The Huffington Post (Feb. 26 2017)

Now. Tomorrow. And the Day After
The Huffington Post (Jan. 12, 2017)

Joyless Justice: The Death Penalty and the Charleston Church Murderer
The Huffington Post (Jan. 10, 2017)

Abundant Love: The Wisdom of Jacob
myjewishlearning.com (Jan. 6, 2017)

This We Do Not Bless: Reach Higher, Rabbi Hier
The Times of Israel (Jan. 3, 2017)

Anger in a Pre-Trump American Zionist: A Rabbinic Response to the Obama Administration's UN Abstention
The Huffington Post (Dec. 28, 2016)

We Don't Have the Words (Ki Tavo)
The Times of Israel (Sept. 22, 2016)

This Election: The Difference Between Terence Crutcher and You
The Huffington Post (Sept. 21, 2016)

We Must Elect Hillary Clinton as President of the United States
The Huffington Post (Aug. 25, 2016)

Gold Gestapo Gun is Headed to Auction
The Jewish Daily Forward (August 17, 2016)

Jerusalem Sits Alone: Tisha Be'Av at the Olympics
Times of Israel (Aug. 12, 2016)

A Wounded Friend: A Rabbinic Response to the New Black Lives Matter Platform
The Huffington Post (Aug. 5, 2016)

No Room for Hate in America
The Huffington Post (July 19, 2016)

Channeling the power of Faith to End Gun Violence
with Eileen Soffer
The Jewish Daily Forward (July 18, 2016)

Choose life, says Torah — not guns
with Eileen Soffer
J Weekly (July 14, 2016)

A Note from Camp Ramah, A Heart In Israel
The Huffington Post (July 6, 2016)

The Eyes of Chovav (BeHa'alotecha)
The Times of Israel (May 31, 2016)

How Bend the Arc is Fighting Donald Trump
The Jewish Daily Forward (May 22, 2016)

Our Testimony: A Yom HaShoah Message
The Times of Israel (May 5, 2016)

These Are Dark Days for America
The Huffington Post Politics (May 3, 2016)

The Way Forward
Sh'ma Journal (April 15, 2016)

Yearning Americans: A Prayer for a Beloved Society
offered at the US Capitol Building as part of the Fact
Coalition/JubileeUSA Tax and Transparency Days
April 11, 2016

Our Ancestors in Heaven Are Weeping
Rabbi Creditor's AIPAC Policy Conference 2016 Address
(March 22, 2016)

*Applause, applause, applause: Donald Trump isn't the problem,
we are*
Times of Israel (March 22, 2016)

*Opposing Trump at AIPAC Is No Partisan Stance — It's Jewish
and All-American Patriotism*
The Jewish Daily Forward (March 21, 2016)

No Time for Neutrality, No Time for Hate (video)
YouTube (March 16, 2016)

*Now is No Time for Neutrality: We Must Stop Trump Before It's
Too Late*
The Huffington Post Politics (March 14, 2016)

Open to Wonder: Parashat #Pekudei
Times of Israel (February 29, 2016)

Success at the Kotel Comes at a Cost
Times of Israel (February 2, 2016)

Must it be Armageddon?
Times of Israel (January 7, 2016)

An Intention for Hope in the New Year
Huffington Post Religion (Dec. 29, 2015)

The Threat of Serenity
Huffington Post Religion (Nov. 30, 2015)

Black Lives Matter and the Beauty of Israel: Working on Both with One Soul
Huffington Post Politics (Nov. 25, 2015)

Bound and Blessed (Again) (Toldot)
Times of Israel (November 10, 2015)

The Blessed Burden (Chayei Sarah)
Times of Israel (November 2, 2015)

Silence: A Blessing or a Danger?
with Shalom Bayit Executive Director Naomi Tucker
J Weekly (Oct. 23, 2015)

A Real Response to Israel-Hatred: Love
Huffington Post Politics (Oct. 22, 2015)

Praying for Israel During Troubled Times
Huffington Post Politics (October 14, 2015)

This is Not a Million Man March
Times of Israel (October 12, 2015)

Alone, Together (Yom Kippur 2015)
Times of Israel (September 24, 2015)

Falafel Hebrew, Crackling Tanks, and Burning Coals
Times of Israel (July 13, 2015)

'A girl named Jerusalem: Seeking Asylum in Tel Aviv
Times of Israel (July 7, 2015)

Too Busy Protecting Israel from Delegitimization to Protect Ourselves from Israel's Delegitimization of Us?
Times of Israel (July 5, 2015)

Our Broken Society, My Broken Heart: A Rabbi on a Jury
J Weekly (June 18, 2015)

We Must Rebuild God's House by Saving Each Other's: A Spiritual Response to Charleston
Huffington Post (June 18, 2015)

The Rabbinic Imperative to Confront American Gun Violence
Times of Israel (June 11, 2015)

Becoming Neighbors: A Jewish Vision of Social Justice
Huffington Post (June 8, 2015)

Gun Violence is a Moral Problem
Huffington Post (April 20, 2015)

For Zion's Sake I Will Not Keep Silent
Huffington Post (March 17, 2015)

Money and Shabbat
Huffington Post (February 25, 2014)

No Rest for the Righteous
Times of Israel (December 8, 2014)

After a Rainstorm of Voter Disenfranchisement in 2014, Congress Must Restore the Voting Rights Act
co-authored with Bend the Arc CEO Stosh Cotler
Roll Call (November 20, 2014)

We Cry as Family
Times of Israel (November 18, 2014)

The Uncertain Woods of Faith
Huffington Post (October 26, 2014)

Ferguson is Not Gaza
Huffington Post Politics Blog (October 15, 2014)

Why Rabbi Gil Steinlauf's Coming Out is a Watershed Moment for Jews
The Jewish Daily Forward (October 7, 2014)

The Burdens of Memory
Times of Israel (October 6, 2014)

White Robes and Infinity
Times of Israel (October 2, 2014)

Intense Beginnings
Huffington Post (September 14, 2014)

A Battered People Once Again
Times of Israel (August 27, 2014)

Ferguson and Israel
Huffington Post (August 21, 2014)

Never Again is Right Now
Times of Israel (August 20, 2014)

Pro-Israel, Pro-Peace
Times of Israel (August 9, 2014)

My Response to the Terror of Missiles and the Terror of Words
Times of Israel (August 4, 2014)

Comfort Our People, Compassion for All God's People
(with Rabbi Michael Adam Latz)
Huffington Post (July 30, 2014)

Do We Stand With Israel?
Huffington Post (July 28, 2014)

The End of Theory
Times of Israel (July 22, 2014)

I'm Done Apologizing for Israel
Huffington Post (July 21, 2014)
(republished by the Jewish Forward July 23, 2014)

The Jewish People Lives
Huffington Post (July 8, 2014)

A Jewish Perspective on Taxes, Poverty
Courier Post (July 3, 2014)

A Jew in the World
Huffington Post, (July 2, 2014)

Army of Angels needed to right tax, poverty woes
The Daily Journal, (June 19, 2014)

On Father' Day, let's End Violence Against Women
The Forward, (June 15, 2014)

We are the Conservative Movement, Fighting for You. It's Your Turn to Stand Up for Us Too
(*in Hebrew*) Maariv (June 10, 2014)

Healing Our Abused Jewish Soul
Jerusalem Post (June 2, 2014)

A Rabbi's Heart Beats Again
Huffington Post (May 16, 2014)

Children in the Sanctuary
Huffington Post (May 5, 2014)

Sarah Palin's Heresy
Huffington Post (April 30, 2014)

Expectations, Despair, and Amazement
Huffington Post (April 25, 2014)

Human Boundaries and Inclusion
Huffington Post (April 4, 2014)

The Promise of Redistribution
Huffington Post (March 28, 2014)

Jews and Gun Violence: An Update
Huffington Post (March 14, 2014)

First Kisses, Intimacy, and Eternity
Huffington Post (March 12, 2014)

Wrong on 'Partnership Minyanim'
Letter to the New York Jewish Week (March 5, 2014)

In Search of Concern
Letter to the New York Times (Feb. 23, 2014)

Leadership: Always for and Sometimes Within
Huffington Post (Feb. 7, 2014)

"We Believe" - in Ending Violence Against Women
JWeekly (Feb. 7, 2014)

A Rabbinic Comment on Messianic Politics
Huffington Post (January 22, 2014)

What Does it Mean?
Huffington Post (January 15, 2014)

Shabbat, a Cellphone, and Jewish Concern
Huffington Post (January 7, 2014)

A Rabbinic Riff on Capitalism (inspired by J.K. Rowling)
Huffington Post (December 31, 2013)

A Rabbi's Christmas Thought (for Jewish Parents and Others)
Huffington Post (December 23, 2013)

Channukah & Thanksgiving: It's Complicated
Huffington Post (November 28, 2013)

Progress from Process
Zeek (November 4, 2013)

Dark Wisdom: A Jewish Comment on the Conclusion of Breaking Bad
Huffington Post (September 30, 2013)

Sukkot Holiday Dvar Tzedek: Ushpizin
American Jewish World Service (Sukkot 2013)

Restoring the Arc (of A Love Affair
Huffington Post (September 16, 2013)

The Eyes Have It
Huffington Post (September 9, 2013)

All That Matters
Sh'ma: A Journal of Jewish Responsibility (September 2013)

What's So High About the High Holidays?
JWeekly (Aug. 29, 2013)

haYom Harat olam // Today the World is Born: a Kavanah on Saving Lives
JCPA (Rosh haShannah 2013)

Wholeness and Sacrifice: Circumcision, Mutuality, Trees and Quilts
Huffington Post (August 12, 2013)

Reclaiming Zionism
Huffington Post (July 8, 2013)

I am Not Free When My Sister is Silenced
Women of the Wall (July 8, 2013)

Sadly, Conservative Judaism's lead ship is sinking fast
JWeekly (June 20, 2013)

Eternity Can Wait
Huffington Post (June 19, 2013)

Found: A Jewish Reflection on Lost
Huffington Post (June 10, 2013)

Legacy and Family: A Hadran for Harry Potter
Huffington Post (May 28, 2013)

What is it about Bedtime?
Huffington Post (May 20, 2013)

"A Prayer for Direction", "A Prayer for Health", and "A Prayer for Travel"
in Jewish Men Pray (Jewish Lights, 2013, ed. Olitzky and Matlins)

Dynamic Connections: The Theology of 'The Runaway Bunny'
Huffington Post (May 9, 2013)

A Prayer, Upon Completing My Term as CoChair of Rabbis for Women of the Wall
Women of the Wall (April 28, 2013)

Be Like Busch: An Open Letter to the NRA Membership
(with Rabbi Aaron Alexander, Rabbi Sharon Brous, & Rabbi Ronit Tsadok)
Huffington Post (April 23, 2013)

A Kavanah Before Eating Fair-Trade Chocolate (Passover)
Fair Trade Judaica (March 2013)

Wandering Toward a Promised Land
Sh'ma: A Journal of Jewish Responsibility (Jan.2013)

A Prayer in Wake of a School Shooting
The Rabbinical Assembly (Dec. 14, 2012)

A Kavanah Before Eating Fair-Trade Chocolate (Channukah)
Fair Trade Judaica (Nov. 2012)

A Prayer in the Aftermath of a Devastating Storm
The Rabbinical Assembly (Oct. 31, 2012)

Heed the Call to End Modern Slavery in Our Own Backyard
The "J" (Sept. 27, 2012)

A Purim Dvar Torah on Gay and Lesbian Recognition (with Rabbi Steven Greenberg)
KeshetOnline (2012)

Within our Hearts: The Holy of Holies
Sh'ma: A Journal of Jewish Responsibility (March, 2012)

Shmot 2012: "A World Without Children's Voices"
The Daily Rabbi (January 2012)

Yes, An Orthodox Rabbi Can 'Do' a Commitment Ceremony
(with Rabbi Jason Miller)
The Huffington Post (December 16, 2011)

Sermon on the Mount: A Midrash on the Akeidah
Sh'ma: A Journal of Jewish Responsibility (August, 2011)

Jews and Others: A Conversation with JTS Chancellor Arnold Eisen
JTS Conservative Judaism Blog (August, 2011)

Upon the Death of an Enemy
The Daily Rabbi (May 2, 2011)

Kedoshim: Intense and Holy
The Daily Rabbi (April 2011)

I am Not You: An Exchange of Letters (with Rabbi Stuart Kelman)
Sh'ma: A Journal of Jewish Responsibility (January, 2011)

Righteousness, Justice, and Reuben Fulfilled
Truah: Rabbis for Human Rights (December, 2010)

The Choice to Include
JewsByChoice.org (Nov. 16, 2010)

Zionism Also Needs to Come from the Left - Right?
The "J" (Nov. 4, 2010)

Safe Jewish Homes
Conversations: The Journal of the Institute for Jewish Ideas and Ideals
(Issue 8; Autumn 2010/5771; "Orthodoxy and Ethics")

The Narrowing of the Israeli Mindset
The "J" (March 4, 2010)

The Necessity of Windows
chapter in Torah Queeries (NYU, 2009)

Living in the Dream: An Integrated Life
Walking with Life: The Ziegler School of Rabbinic Studies (Summer 2009)

Conservative Judaism and Denominationalism
Gevanim: The Journal of the Academy of Jewish Religion (Vol. 5, Summer 2009)

The Revelation of an Embrace: A Vision of Conservative Judaism
Conservative Judaism (Vol. 61, Fall/Winter 2008-09)

Creating Spiritual Prayer
CJ: Voices of Conservative/Masorti Judaism (Fall 2008)

Marriage Ruling is About Universal Human Dignity
The "J" (May 23, 2008)

Toward a Hopeful Judaism
The New York Jewish Week (3/3/07)

In Defense of Jingle Bells
The New York Jewish Week (12/22/06)

God's Loneliness
Jewels of Elul II (Summer 2006)

Sustained Innovation
Sh'ma: A Journal of Jewish Responsibility (June 2006)

Pesach: Excessive Freedom
The UJC Rabbinic Orchard (Spring 2005)

White Robes and Infinity
The UJC Rabbinic Orchard (Fall 2004)

Parashat VaYeira: Seeing the Other
Sh'ma: A Journal of Jewish Responsibility

Akeidat haMa'achelet / The Binding of the Knife
Living Text: The Journal of Contemporary Midrash (1999, Vol #5)

Books, edited or authored, by Menachem Creditor

Not By Might: Channeling the power of Faith to End Gun Violence (2016)

And Yet We Love: Poems (2016)

Primal Prayers: Spiritual Responses to a Real World (2015)

The Hope: American Jewish Voices in Support of Israel (2014)

Commanded to Live: One Rabbi's Reflections on Gun Violence (2014)

Siddur Tov LeHodot (Shabbat Morning Transliterated Prayerbook) (2013)

Thanksgiving Torah: Jewish Reflections on an American Holiday (2013)

A Manifesto for the Future: The ShefaNetwork Archive: Conservative/Masorti Judaism Dreaming from Within (2013)

Peace in Our Cities: Rabbis Against Gun Violence (2013)

Slavery, Freedom, and Everything Between: The Why, How and What of Passover (2013) co-edited with Aaron Alexander

A Pesach Rhyme (2012)

Avodah: A Yom Kippur Story (2012)

Rabbi Rebecca and the Thanksgiving Leftovers (2012)

Rabbi Menachem Creditor (@rabbicreditor) is spiritual leader of Congregation Netivot Shalom in Berkeley, CA, and the founder of Rabbis Against Gun Violence. Named by Newsweek as one of the 50 most influential rabbis in America, he is a regular contributor to The Huffington Post and The Times of Israel. He is a founding Board Member of the Movement for One America.

He has authored and edited thirteen books, including *Not By Might: Rabbis Against Gun Violence* (2016), *And Yet We Love: Poems* (2016), *Primal Prayers* (2015), *The Hope: American Jewish Voices in Support of Israel* (2014), *Peace in Our Cities* (2013), and *Siddur Tov LeHodot: A Transliterated Shabbat Morning Prayerbook* (2012). His children's books include *Rabbi Rebecca and the Thanksgiving Leftovers, Avodah: A Yom Kippur Story* and *A Pesach Rhyme*.

A frequent speaker on Jewish Leadership and Literacy in communities around the United States and Israel, he has served as a Trustee of American Jewish World Service, Shalom Bayit, and sits on the Social Justice Commission of the International Rabbinical Assembly.

Find out more at menachemcreditor.net.